# COUNTRY STORES *of*

# MISSISSIPPI

JUNE DAVIS DAVIDSON

*Foreword by Dr. Roy McNeill*

Charleston  London

THE
History
PRESS

Published by The History Press
Charleston, SC 29403
www.historypress.net

*Back cover, mid-left*: This potbellied stove is the Simmons-Wright Company's only source of heat. The heater has been in use at the store for almost one hundred years. Pictured is Bobby Davidson. *Courtesy of the author.*

First published 2014

Manufactured in the United States

ISBN 978.1.62619.592.9

Library of Congress CIP data applied for.

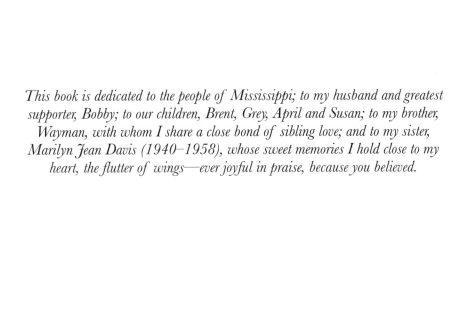

*This book is dedicated to the people of Mississippi; to my husband and greatest supporter, Bobby; to our children, Brent, Grey, April and Susan; to my brother, Wayman, with whom I share a close bond of sibling love; and to my sister, Marilyn Jean Davis (1940–1958), whose sweet memories I hold close to my heart, the flutter of wings—ever joyful in praise, because you believed.*

# CONTENTS

# FOREWORD

By trade, I am an English teacher. Although I've been out of the classroom for fifteen years, I still introduce myself that way. Strangely enough, I almost wasn't an English teacher; I was almost a history teacher. On the day I declared my major to my university advisor, I was primed and ready to embark on a college career that would ultimately conclude with me teaching Mississippi history in front of a group of high school freshmen or searching for Civil War relics in the fields around Vicksburg (dressed like Indiana Jones, of course) when in a moment of youthful rebellion I blurted out "English" as my major instead. In truth, I was torn between my love for powerful language and literature and my fascination with the places and people who lived those stories I loved to read. Reading June Davidson's *Country Stores of Mississippi* reminded me of that early collegiate struggle in my soul. The wonder of those places that our ancestors frequented, where they worked and bought and where they shared love and grief and hopes and dreams and, above all, stories, thrills me. After reading about each old country store, I am left envisioning myself sitting on the porch whittling and swapping stories or drinking glass bottles of Coke with a slice of hoop cheese, and part of me hurts because my life didn't turn in such a direction as to study the lives and times of those folks who did.

Fortunately, I have June Davidson to tell me about those people and places. While it might not quite be the same as dressing up as Indiana Jones and using a toothbrush to dust off some long-buried but recently unearthed Mississippi antiquity, reading June's book fills my heart and mind with all the information and imagination of those days gone by without the ill-fitting clothes. I can't find a fedora that looks good on me anyway. So for now, I'll curl up in my recliner with that accursed television muted and read about the Mississippi of my father, my grandfather and his father, the Mississippi where, were it not for a few years, I might be living, the sweetness of which can leap off the pages and take shape in my imagination because I didn't have to live the difficulties associated with it and because of June's word pictures. I can't return to the Mississippi of yesteryear and sit on those porches with my hoop cheese in hand, but reading *Country Stores of Mississippi* certainly makes me feel as if I am there and inspires within me an aching, echoing longing that I could have been. If you love Mississippi like I do, if you love history like I do, you'll read this one again and again. In doing so, you'll be reminded as I am that, although I'm not on that porch today, I was in the person of my father and his fathers—and how sweet it is to visit.

DR. ROY MCNEILL

# ACKNOWLEDGEMENTS

I would like to thank those who gave of their time and family photographs; without you, many stories would have been left untold. A special thank-you to Dr. Roy McNeill and Lydia Dell, whose love for old country stores encouraged my journey.

# INTRODUCTION

In the early fall of 2013, my travels on the back roads of Mississippi in search of old country stores had come to an end, and as I left the Delta, a full moon danced over cotton fields that stretched across the landscape in a sea of white. My mind wandered back to another time. They were mental images of the past, of history long buried in Mississippi soil.

My travels across the rural part of the state have brought much pleasure, and the images of rural communities will remain as special memories. The Mississippi back roads I traveled always led me home.

With a total of 48,434 square miles of territory in Mississippi, it is impossible to find each community and historic country store that served it. There are many stories left untold, and I regret those I missed. It is these rural settlements, too, that gave our state a solid foundation to build on.

Let us not forget, we hold in our hands a treasure more precious than gold—freedom. A gift of immeasurable wealth left to us by our forefathers, it must be protected and nurtured, loved and respected for this and future generations.

It is my hope that by preserving a part of Mississippi's rural history, future generations will be proud of their heritage and of the settlers who formed our communities and our towns.

Mississippi is a land rich in resources that bounds a great river on the eastern shore; it is territory once fought over by France, Spain and England. It is here, along the banks of the mighty Mississippi River, that the history of Mississippi begins.

# THE MISSISSIPPI RIVER

## A FLUID THOROUGHFARE TO THE GULF

History does not tell us their number, but rather the bones of men scattered along Mississippi's three-hundred-mile Native American footpath tell us of the dangers that lurked along it. Many of the travelers were boatmen who came by flatboats down the Mississippi River to Fort Rosalie's trading post.[1]

Fort Rosalie, known today as Natchez, is the location of one of the first trading posts in the Mississippi territory. This fort was built by Governor Jean Baptiste Le Moyne de Bienville with the aid of the Natchez Indians in 1716.[2]

The Natchez Indians, a warring tribe of sun worshipers, attacked Fort Rosalie in 1729 and slaughtered most of the inhabitants under French rule. The French counterattacked, and the surviving members of the Natchez tribe fled and joined other tribes.[3]

Fur and pelt traders floated down the Mississippi River to the trading post at Fort Rosalie.[4] Flatboats did not travel upriver because of strong currents. Instead, boatmen traveled home by a footpath created by Native Americans hundreds of years ago.[5]

Many of these traders never survived the trek back home. They were robbed and killed by bandits who lay in wait along the trail or died from other causes. The traders who did survive lived off wild game from the lush forest abundant with oak and hickory. They followed the path northward where it lay covered with fallen pine needles and the air was filled with the crisp, clean fragrance of pine. The traders' footsteps led them down a path where waterfalls and springs had quenched the thirst of the thousands whose footsteps had walked this trail before them through virgin forest where men listened to the mournful coo of a dove at twilight that filled their hearts with loneliness.

Regardless of the dangers they faced, these traders enjoyed a lucrative fur and pelt trade, one that met the demand from merchandisers in France. It is this demand, perhaps, that led to more trading posts and settlements across Mississippi.[6]

The birth of the mighty Mississippi River begins as a five-foot-deep body of water at Lake Itasca in Minnesota and flows 2,350 miles southward to the mouth of the Gulf of Mexico.[7] The river, fed by its tributaries, becomes a mighty warrior, an untamed body of water that divides a nation, the East from the West.

The Mississippi River played a crucial role in the development of a young country, a liquid transportation route that led from northern Minnesota to the Gulf of Mexico. The river and territory has been fought over by the French, Spanish and English from the early 1700s to the last quarter of that century, when Patrick Henry's rallying cry—"Give me liberty, or give me death"—echoed throughout the colonies in their fight for independence from England, a conflict won in 1776 that gave birth to a new nation, America.

## 2

# EARLY SETTLEMENTS IN THE MISSISSIPPI TERRITORY

Louis Lefleur, a French Canadian trader, married Rebecca Cravett, the niece of a Choctaw chief named Pushmataha, who was "the eagle of his tribe, with war paint in his words, if not on his face and a tomahawk in his logic."[8] Louis Lefleur established a trading post during the colonial period at Lefleur Bluff on the banks of the Pearl River before 1817. Lefleur Bluff is now known as Jackson. He later returned to the Choctaw Nation and settled at what is now known as French Camp and established a trading post.[9]

When new trading posts were established in the Mississippi Territory, new settlements began to develop nearby.

Northeast of Natchez, Robert H. Bell operated an Indian trading post at the junction of Natchez Trace and Old Vicksburg Road during the late 1700s. Pierre Juzan traded with the Choctaws at his trading post due east at Chunky Chitto before the removal of Native Americans from the Mississippi Territory in 1830.[10]

This is the same year that John Williams established a trading post at Williams' Landing on the Yazoo River. Williams' Landing incorporated in 1844 as Greenwood. Both the county and town are named for Greenwood Lefleur, the son of Louis Lefleur. Greenwood later changed his surname to Leflure.[11]

Early trading posts were often located near waterways where trappers sold or traded hides or furs for goods at a settlement trading post. Often, these posts were established to trade with Native Americans, although many of these early settlements would become extinct by the late 1800s. Nevertheless, the mid-1800s would bring about change as more rural settlements were established in Mississippi.

Jefferson Davis Dickenson, in an effort to preserve Fort Rosalie's history, re-created the fort in 1940 by using hand-hewed logs at the original location of the fort.[12] The pentagon-shaped structure and outbuildings were built at the original location of Fort Rosalie. The National Park Service purchased this parcel of land, and it is now part of the National Parks system.

The trading posts of the 1700s and early 1800s gave way to general mercantile stores that were privately owned. These stores were the provider of farm supplies, clothing and staples to rural farm families. In addition to the general mercantile store, many owners operated cotton gins and gristmills on their premises.

By the mid-1900s, the old country stores were fading from Mississippi's landscape and giving way to the modern-day convenience store found on street corners in small towns across Mississippi.

From one of Mississippi Territory's first known trading posts at Fort Rosalie to the modern convenience store of today, the old country stores and the communities they served allow us to experience a part of history by joining the past with the present.

## 3

# THE INVISIBLE LINE THAT
# DIVIDED A NATION

From the first gunshot at Fort Sumter, South Carolina, on April 12, 1861, the war for Southern independence spread across a divided nation—the North from the South—separated by an invisible line: the Mason-Dixon line.

The Confederacy was formed in February 1861 under the leadership of Jefferson Davis, the only person to serve as president in the Confederate government. Many who were loyal to the Confederacy objected to the practice of sending a substitute to serve in the Confederate military. This became a concern for President Jefferson Davis, and he signed a bill (S. 142) that prohibited substitute replacements.[13]

In 1863, the Confederate House of Representatives approved a bill (H.R. 79) that prohibited the use of Federal paper money.[14] Because of this law, staunch supporters of the Confederacy whose rich coffers were once plentiful with Confederate money would become paupers, holders of worthless paper at the end of the war.

While General William Tecumseh Sherman marched across Mississippi with his torch and band of looting marauders, homes and businesses were left in ashes; railroads ties lay twisted, creating a temporary halt on rail movement of Confederate troops and munitions.

General Ulysses Grant rendezvoused with Admiral David Porter in Tennessee and ferried twenty-four thousand Union troops down the Mississippi past Vicksburg under a hail of cannon fire. Grant marched northward through Port Gibson and then veered toward Jackson, with his ultimate goal as Mississippi's last line of defense for the Confederacy:

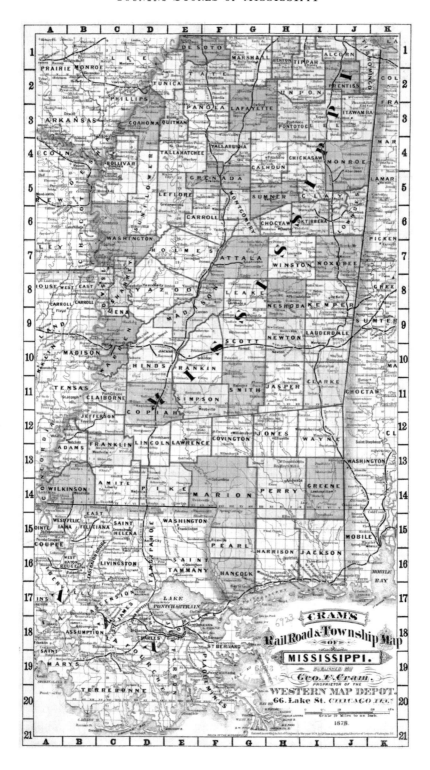

Vicksburg. Federal boats moored nearby fired cannons over the city that sat on a two-hundred-foot bluff while Union forces advanced. Seventy thousand Union forces waited to attack the Confederacy stronghold, which was under the command of John C. Pemberton's Confederate headquarters on Crawford Street.

Frightened women and children fled to caves as cannon fire raged over Vicksburg until General Ulysses Grant captured the ragged and starved Confederate town on July 4, 1864. The scars of battle still visible from cannonballs act as reminders, and it would be well into the twentieth century before Vicksburg would celebrate July Fourth as Independence Day.

The hardship of Reconstruction began when unscrupulous carpetbaggers entered the state. Corruption soon followed with higher property taxes that caused once valuable land to fall into the hands of carpetbaggers, whom some Southerners considered the scourge of the South. Former slaves were elected to represent the state, and plantation owners began the practice of sharecropping that included housing, seed and farming implements being furnished to the sharecropper for a share of the profit at the end of the harvest season.

The plantation commissary was born of this practice, a system in which each participant had a commissary account that was used to provide necessities for sharecroppers until the end of harvest season, a time when the commissary account bill would be due.

On February 23, 1870, Congress readmitted Mississippi to the Union.[15] And this is the brief history of settlements and a war-torn South that led to general stores in rural communities built near waterways in Mississippi's virgin forests. From farmland to industrialization, the region has grown by magnificent proportions.

*Opposite*: Map of Mississippi in 1878. *Courtesy of National Archives.*

# MISSISSIPPI

## OASIS IN THE WILDERNESS

A fter the war, the trading posts of the 1700s and early 1800s gave way to the general mercantile stores that were the provider of farm supplies, clothing and staples to rural farm families. In addition to the general mercantile store, many owners operated cotton gins and gristmills on their premises.

Most communities were located near waterways. The church and general store became important parts of Mississippi's rural communities during this era when work began at dawn and ended when the veil of darkness fell across the sky. Life, like the old adage, held true: "A man works from sunup to sundown, but a woman's work is never done."

They made shirts and dresses from flour sacks and quilts from colorful scraps of material that were stuffed with cotton for warmth. They boiled laundry in iron wash pots and hung it outdoors to dry. They pressed clothes with a flat iron heated in the hot coals of a fireplace, summer and winter. They cooked on a wood stove three times a day, canned vegetables from the garden and nursed the infants they bore year after year. Men traveled by mule and wagon, hunted wild game and taught sons to do the same. They used home remedies for sickness and relied on prayers and faith to heal.

They were families who were self-sufficient, with a strong belief in biblical doctrine. They were the men and women who were dismissed from church rolls for dancing, gossiping, fighting, gambling or drinking liquor and with repentance and public church apology were reinstated as members in good standing. They farmed and helped neighbors in times of need, and they came together as a community of one whose faith in the Gospel was the building block of family life.

# THE HISTORY OF COUNTRY STORES IN MISSISSIPPI

## LAUDERDALE COUNTY

The Choctaw Nation held a strong presence in the red clay hills of this county until a division of land occurred in 1817, when the Mississippi and Alabama Territories were divided. Mississippi, granted statehood that same year, allotted 750 square miles of this land to create Lauderdale County, named for a Virginian, Colonel James Lauderdale, a capable military man destined to die in the War of 1812.

Choctaw villages diminished in Lauderdale County after the 1830 Treaty of Dancing Rabbit Creek. The small pre–Civil War village of Sowashee changed its name to Meridian and captured the railroad destination, as well as the county seat, from Marion Station. By 1890, Meridian had become the largest city in Mississippi.

The turbulent history of the county has spanned over 180 years. It survived the yellow fever epidemic, the Civil War, Reconstruction, riots and the 1916 tornado that decimated a portion of Meridian.

And so it was in 1860, when R.S. Raynor built a trading post in the wilderness and a community grew and thrived, in part because of men like Raynor and T.J. Bostick, a merchant and lumberman.[16] For 153 years, a portion of this trading post has been in existence. Today, this community is known as Causeyville.

## E.W. Hagwood General Store

Meander down one of many country roads across Mississippi and look for the state's hidden gem, the old country store. The Causeyville Road in Lauderdale County, once a trail traveled by mule and wagon, will lead you directly to the old Raynor trading post and the E.W. Hagwood General Store, now known as Causeyville General Store, erected in 1895. These are two of the oldest country stores in the county.

Drive past the plantation-style home and follow the winding country road sprinkled with blackberry bushes nestled among flowering magnolias, fragrant pines and sweet gum trees. When you arrive, a large hand-painted Coca-Cola sign splashed across the building will greet you. Step inside, and your senses will come to life as fans stir the air with the aroma of roasting peanuts in a restored 1890s peanut roaster.

Near the door sits a Coca-Cola chest from a bygone era filled with ice and bottled soft drinks. Tease your taste buds with a sample of mellow hoop cheese, sliced by the store's cheese cutter that has been used for over one hundred years, or sit on the nearby wooden loafer's bench tucked under the window or in the old red barber chair nestled in the corner.

The E.W. Hagwood General Store, built in 1895, is now known as the Causeyville General Store. The building once included a voting precinct, physician's office, movie theater and post office. *Courtesy of the author.*

You might find Dorothy Hagwood, the proprietor, in conversation with visitors. Her hands paint a picture visible only to the mind's eye. Dorothy's southern drawl glides easily above the hum of ceiling fans with tales of the store's ghostly inhabitants and sightings of Babe, her faithful Great Dane. Dorothy gives credit to Babe for saving her life on at least two occasions during attempted robberies.

Peek over the counter, and you're likely to see Girl, a blond, shaggy-haired dog sprawled on the floor behind the counter. Girl's days of youth and foxhunts are long past. She is now content to lumber slowly around waiting for her next meal.

The mill store and gristmill located next door to Causeyville General Store were built by R.S. Raynor in 1860. He sold dry goods, tobacco, hardware, groceries, turpentine, patent medicine and rough and finished lumber that he milled. This building served as a trading post for settlers and Choctaw Indians after the Civil War and during Reconstruction. Choctaw medicine men from Alamuchee sold herbal medicine, tonics and tribal remedies at the general store.[17]

In 1895, T.J. Bostick and Jim Smith built the present-day general store, and the old store became a cotton warehouse. At the Mill Shop, a hand-

The T.J. Bostick & Sons Trading Post is located on Causeyville Road next to the Causeyville General Store. *Courtesy of Dorothy Hagwood.*

cranked gas pump pumped fuel up into a clear glass cylinder, etched with gallons. The attached fuel hose flowed gas by gravity.

By 1910, T.J. Bostick had sold his store to Joe (Joseph) Grantham, who would remain the store proprietor for the next thirty-two years.

If you could turn back the pages of history and sit on Grantham's porch, you would see farmers loading buggies with staples and perhaps hear the sounds of a neighing horse, eager to be loose from its hitching post. Or you could watch women in calico dresses, their long tresses swept upward and knotted into a bun secured by a single long pin, admire the ribbons and bows they purchased to adorn hand-sewn clothes. Farmers clad in overalls, clay clinging to their boot soles, left a trail of red dirt behind as the screen door opened, screeched and shuddered close on rusty hinges.

This was an era when an acre of land often sold for a bale of cotton, with payment due at harvest, a time when farm families often bartered with eggs, chickens and produce for goods at the country store.

By the 1920s, the store contained a soda fountain, the post office and Dr. Billy's office. Dr. William J. "Billy" Anderson, a former postmaster for Increase (the town's former name) and gin and sawmill operator, attended medical school and practiced medicine in a small alcove inside the store. He made house calls on horseback before he purchased a Model T Ford. He had been referred to in the community as Dr. Billy, a physician who often received payment in poultry or vegetables for medical services. Area residents give credit to Dr. Anderson for the first telephone exchange in the community.

"Dr. Billy," ninety-year-old Lucy Carter, a longtime resident of the Causeyville area, said, "was the spoke that made the wheel turn in the community."

Between 1932 and 1933, Causeyville was a thriving community served by a church, a doctor, a two-story school and two general stores. During this time period, the ledger book of Mosley's General Store in Snell, an adjoining community in Clarke County, noted that the store sold smoking tobacco for five cents, a mule for sixty-five dollars and denim overalls for fifty cents.[18]

The store's ownership changed again in 1942 during World War II when Everett W. Hagwood bought the Grantham house, store and mill from the Granthams.[19]

"Both stores have been in our family for over 70 of a 116-year history," Joanne Hagwood Culpepper said. "When my brother, Leslie, was twelve or thirteen years old, at his insistence, Daddy bought him a movie projector. Leslie bought church pews from a church in the Energy community. In the summer, Leslie used the pews for movie seats in the open field beside our house. We watched movies on bed sheets pinned to the clothesline. In the

Causeyville General Store is nine miles south of Meridian. T.J. Bostick and Jim Smith built the store in 1898. *Courtesy of the author.*

winter months, movies were shown in the rear of the store," Joanne said. "Leslie screened movies to white people on Friday nights, then black people on Saturday nights. That's just the way it was back then."

Joanne Hagwood Irby leased the store to Jack and Merrelese Tedder and then later to Ralph and Martha Germany before Leslie Hagwood Sr. purchased the store.

Step to the back of the store, and you will find an array of player pianos. The old Wurlitzer nickelodeon from the twenties required a nickel to play a recorded tune. A sixty-four-note piano and a piano and pipe organ, inset with delicate stained glass, line the back walls amid antique radios, record players, clocks and movie posters.

The most fragile of the store's memorabilia are stored in glass cases. In fact, every nook and cranny of the Causeyville General Store is filled with relics of American history. From antique signs displaying fifteen-cents-a-gallon gas to World War II posters and from Royal Crown Cola and Moon Pies to the days of gas rations and coupons, you'll find these mementos of these days long since past scattered throughout the store.

"After my husband and I bought the store and house from my father, we lived in the Grantham house," Joanne said. "My son, Vance, and mother avoided the former bedroom of Granny Grantham. She died in the bedroom, and Vance and mother would often see Mrs. Grantham's empty chair rocking. Doors would slam closed, caused by a draft in the center hall, but Vance thought otherwise and refused to stay in the house alone."

Then in the early 1980s, Joanne sold the store to her brother, Leslie. Leslie and his wife, Dorothy, worked diligently to restore and preserve the two historic buildings.

### The Unexplained

Caroline Smith, a part-time store clerk during the 1980s, said, "When the store is quiet, I sometimes hear snoring."

Mr. Bostick once resided in the rear of the Causeyville General Store and was known to snore, even while napping during the day.

"I always used care when stacking cans in the corner, and without warning or just 'cause, the cans would crash to the floor, scatter and roll only to be picked up and stacked again," Leslie Hagwood Jr. said.

"Sometimes, I would open the store and find cans of food in the floor," Caroline Smith said. "And I often would hear footsteps in the store when it was empty. When I did hear an unusual noise or [see] a sudden flash of light or a darkened spot in the store that shouldn't be there, I would mutter, 'Huh, that's different,' and continue on with the task I was doing at the time."

"I've seen cans flying off the shelf," Dorothy Hagwood said. "This could be from the settlement of the building," she added.

But one would think after 115 years, the foundation would no longer settle so much that it would cause cans to fly off the shelves or cause the heavy lanterns hanging from the ceiling to spin rapidly around as if by their own will.

"My husband knew I loved old things," Sharon Hurt said, "and when we moved to the Causeyville area, we toured the store. When I stepped to the back of the store, I passed through a cold spot, and as strange as it may seem, I had the feeling of a cold hand running up my back. I've never forgotten the experience."

"One morning I opened the store and found a loaf of bread lying on the floor. I picked it up and placed it back on the shelf," Bob, a part-time store clerk, said. "I knew this was just another unexplained incident in the store I've seen or heard. I've often heard the piano playing in the back room on its own accord. Not the barroom kind of music," he said.

Caroline, Dorothy and Leslie Jr. have all witnessed orbs of light floating in the store. Afterward, a paranormal research group verified the orbs during its investigation in February 2006. "These orbs of light are thought to be energy left from the living," Gigi Ahrens of the investigative group explained. It is often said that truth can be stranger than fiction, but it is truth this paranormal group sought when the organization requested an appointment with Dorothy Hagwood to investigate the store's paranormal activity. The findings of the paranormal group, after setting up black lights, audio equipment and still and video cameras in the building for overnight observation, were astounding. A large dust cloud appeared over the player piano, and the audible sneezing from the store's sneezing ghost could be heard; its allergy to dust was made known to the group's audio equipment. The sneezing ghost is thought to be a previous owner who once lived in the back of the store and died there.

During the early 1900s, walls were added to enclose the back of the store for T.J. Bostick's family's residence. To witness the most unusual event requires an overnight stay in the store. If you ever decide to spend the night—with permission from the owner, of course—be prepared because you might just witness paranormal events in the darkened back room.

The paranormal research group's video equipment is not the only source to encounter a piano playing in the back room. Caroline Smith and Bob, another clerk, also heard it one afternoon. "I could hear the piano playing," Caroline said. "I turned it off about an hour earlier after tourists left." She hesitated and said, not too convincingly, "I thought perhaps I didn't push the button down far enough to turn it off completely."

Shortly after the paranormal group completed the investigation, a part-time store clerk arrived at 7:00 a.m. to unlock the door to begin the day's business. The moment the clerk opened the door and stepped inside, both feet froze to the floor. A lantern spun from the ceiling, and a nearby advertisement swirled in rapid motion while the sturdy floor remained motionless beneath the clerk's trembling knees.

"The clerk," Dorothy said, "quickly stepped outside and waited for me to return. She refused to work in the store again."

"I suppose the most unusual occurrence happened to a customer as he sat on the Mill Shop porch with his feet propped on the wood railing to relax," Dorothy said. Dorothy relayed the story to me.

*"I'll never do that again," the customer said, clearly shaken as he stepped inside the door of the general store.*

*"What won't you do again?" Dorothy asked.*

*"I will never sit on that porch again. The window behind me would fly open, slam close, then open and close over and over again," he said.*

*"And no one," he stressed, "was inside the Mill Shop."*

*Dorothy motioned for him to follow. "I have something to show you," she said as she unlocked the door of the Mill Shop and walked over to the window. "This window can't open. It is nailed shut," she said, pointing to the nails.*

*"Nailed shut or not, that window opened and slammed shut the entire time I was on the porch," the customer said.*

"I never saw the gentleman again," Dorothy told me.

"Often I would step outside with Babe," Dorothy continued, "and within a few minutes, I would hear footsteps inside the store. I can't tell you how many times I've gone back in thinking I left customers alone only to find the store empty, just as I left it."

CAUSEYVILLE GENERAL STORE IN THE 1900s

The Mill House resumed operation of its gristmill with its restored International Harvester Mill in the 1980s. The only payment the gristmill and miller received was a portion of the farmer's corn.

The country store provided a loafer's bench where old-timers sat, waiting to engage a customer in conversation and to glean any news the visitor might impart. If you stepped back in time, you would hear Allan Sellers tell of the days in 1928, when men with oxen-drawn carts helped construct the railroad bed that ran from Meridian into Alabama.

He might tell how Jesse James spent the night in the old Coker cabin in Vimville and buried his gold in the hills and hollows near the railroad before galloping off to Enterprise, Mississippi. Leslie Hagwood Sr. would have told you about the Confederates who hid out in caves during the War Between the States, although most of the caves have long since collapsed and are now covered with kudzu. Others might tell of the severe winter when ice one inch thick covered the ground, of those who died of influenza during the winter and the spring flood that followed and how farmers dug trenches to drain farmland to plant crops.

Things do change for the better, some people might say. For in 1966, Lauderdale County voted to go "wet" and allow the sale of taxed liquor. Bob laughed when he heard the news.

"Going wet," he cackled, slapping his soiled khaki cap against his thigh. "What do you mean going wet? It's always been wet. Why, you can siphon it out of the ground anywhere." Even today, a few one-gallon glass jugs are found scattered along a creek bank, left there decades ago by the hurried dismantling of moonshine stills.

The Annual Fall Country Days became popular in Mississippi in the 1980s, and the Causeyville community hosted its own Country Day under the direction of Leslie Hagwood Sr. On a Saturday in early November, Gospel performers sang songs of praise, and dulcimer players strummed away on the loafer's bench at the general store. Lash LaRue, the king of the bullwhip, made his appearance at the request of his good friend Leslie Hagwood.

The old store has been there through much of our history. It has seen the election of President Ulysses S. Grant in 1869, home rule in the South, the date Mississippi was readmitted to the union in 1870, Reconstruction after the War Between the States and the 1898 literacy voting test and poll tax and its repeal. The general store was still thriving in 1919, when women received the right to vote. The store survived the sting of the Great Depression and witnessed the redistricting of voting precincts, the end of segregation and Neil Armstrong's walk on the moon. It has said good-bye to local fallen soldiers who served in World War I, World War II, the Korean War, Vietnam and the present-day war in the Middle East. Visitors from around the globe have passed through the door of this old country store and left with the knowledge that they've had the rare privilege of experiencing the past.

The E.W. Hagwood General Store, known today as Causeyville General Store, is located at 6129 Causeyville Road, approximately nine miles south of Meridian, Mississippi. GPS (global positioning) is not accurate with this address.

## J.B. Gunn General Store
### Topton

In February 1905, Gunn's General Store opened its doors for business in the Topton community of Lauderdale County, ten miles from Union Depot in Meridian. Joseph Thornton Gunn built the store, and he was appointed postmaster on May 22, 1905.[20] He replace Topton's first postmaster, Horace Rushing, who had been appointed by the postal service on January 1, 1890.

Gunn's son, J.B., who was born on April 6, 1884, became the store proprietor, according to Harlan Davis.

A steam-powered cotton gin located behind the store was destroyed by fire in 1936. The cotton gin, rebuilt on the corner of Highway 39 and Cotton

The J.B. Gunn General Store is located on Topton Road in Lauderdale County. The first cotton gin was located behind the store. *Courtesy of Harlan Davis.*

Gin Road, catered to local farmers who brought cotton to the gin by the wagon- and truckload. The gin was dismantled in 1995.

J.B. Gunn's General Store may have been a hangout for one of man's furry friends, a cat on the hunt, but it wasn't the squeak of a mouse that caught the cat's attention that night. The proprietor, bewildered over the recurring robbery that had been occurring in his general store during previous nights, couldn't find the burglar's point of entry—that is, not until he moved a wooden keg inside the store and made the discovery that would solve the perplexing mystery.

The cunning thief had crawled beneath the store and, with a saw, cut a hole in the floor large enough to crawl through. He exited the same way he entered and then pulled the wooden keg over the hole to conceal his entry point. The thief was soon caught. The hole has been patched over with ply board and covered with heavy objects.

The general store and Topton Depot were within a few feet of each other. The train, called the Doodlebug, ferreted passengers to and from Topton and Meridian.

In the 1920s, the Doodlebug brought people from Meridian to the old lake at Topton, which had a camp house. "The old lake on our property had

A carbide light attached to a cord that drops from the ceiling was once used to illuminate the J.B. Gunn General Store before electricity arrived in Topton. *Courtesy of the author.*

been a popular meeting place in Topton for picnics and revelry," Harlan Davis said. The railroad and brick culvert built in 1856 prior to the war still exists, although only the foundation of the depot remains.

More excitement came in 1960, when a stranger landed a plane in a Topton field. The fellow had stolen the plane, along with $32,000 in the

Carolinas. He was captured in Meridian. "The plane, but not the money, was recovered," Harlan Davis said.

An airstrip was built during World War II near Topton to train military pilots from nearby Key Field. The war ended in 1945, and the airstrip was never completed.

It was the Key brothers, Fred and Al, who, in a borrowed plane, the *Ole Miss*, lifted off from Key Field on June 4, 1935, and broke the world record for inflight hours, which was enabled by a refueling system designed by A.D. Hunter, an employee of Soulé Steam Feed Works. The Key brothers landed the Ole Miss on July 1, 1935.

The building remains as a testament to craftsmanship, for its sturdiness—it withstood the onslaught of Hurricane Katrina ninety years later. The storm that devastated Mississippi's coastline also wreaked havoc inland. Katrina's winds hurled their mighty force into Lauderdale County and lifted the store's roof, causing a separation of a corner rear wall before the roof settled back into place in defiance, not defeat, although the storm left a visible crack between the rear joined wall.[21]

By 1990, the general store became a commissary, but the doors of this 109-year-old store is now closed, its history trapped within its walls. Memories of transported Confederate troops through Topton have been swept away, but the store still stands as a reminder of another time and way of life, a simpler time when rural families earned a living from the earth. J.B. Gunn General Store is located on Topton Road.

## Simmons-Wright Company
### Kewanee

Kewanee, whose residents were once cattlemen and famers who shipped cattle and cotton by rail, is a community of gently rolling hills near the Alabama state line in Lauderdale County. The early post office may have been located in Kewanee's Mobile & Ohio (M&O) Railroad Depot. Matthias Riffile was the first known appointment as postmaster, which occurred on October 18, 1865. He was followed by John M. Lowd and, later, Alfred J. Brower on April 21, 1871. Postal service was discontinued on June 27, 1877, and reestablished on December 18, 1882. Other postmasters were Alexander C. Collier followed by Lula McElroy in 1898 and John McElroy in 1916.[22]

The Simmons-Wright Company Store was established in 1884 in Kewanee, Mississippi, near the Alabama state line. The original store

Two sets of screened doors and transom windows help cool the interior of the Simmons-Wright Company Store in the summer. *Courtesy of the author.*

burned in 1926 and was replaced the same year with a modern (for its time) brick store.

The historic general merchandise store was the heart of the Toomsuba and Kewanee communities near the old Dixie Highway. During the early years of the store's long history, William Simmons and Tom Wright depended on local farmers and their cotton crops for the store's survival. Wright and Simmons were progressive men that catered to area farmers' needs. The store supplied farm implements, seeds, clothing and other necessities of the era. A blacksmith shop and cotton gin were part of the store's property. The railroad played a vital role in the community by providing farmers and cattlemen rail transportation for ginned cotton and cattle.

In the early fall, farmers picked cotton, the only cash crop depended on to carry their families from cotton season to cotton season.

One can imagine a farmer, his wagon loaded with cotton, a cloud of dust following behind, as it snaked along the rutted trail. In the distance, the sound of a train whistle cracked out three short blasts. The driver tightened the reins and held his teams of horses steady as he approached the tracks.

The ground shuddered as the train swayed and groaned against steel and puffed a trail of black smoke. The acrid smell of coal burned at the farmer's throat, and he pulled down his hat to protect his eyes from swirling cinders. The stationmaster stood on the platform of Kewanee Depot and gave the all-clear signal to cross the track.

As the driver neared the Simmons-Wright Company Store, he joined a long line of wagons at the cotton gin. The sale of cotton would bring a decent amount, enough for him to clear his debt at Simmons-Wright Company. He was grateful that the store carried farm accounts from season to season. Now, he could use his store account to buy seeds and fertilizer for next season and other necessities for his family.

On March 7, 1906, one can image that Cecil Ryan, preoccupied with Simmons-Wright Company accounts, filtered out the sounds from Samuel Thompson's blacksmith shop. Both men were probably unaware that across the way at the depot, Robert A. Phillips busied himself preparing outgoing mail for the train and C.H. Hopson sent messages over the telegraph while a northbound freight train barreled down the Mobil and Ohio train track in the direct path of the Southbound Limited.

On March 8, 1906, a Birmingham newspaper reported the head-on collision between the Southbound Limited and a northbound freight train in Kewanee that killed six and injured several. The collision caused damage to several nearby homes. Shortly after, Tom Wright married Cornelia, the daughter of William Simmons.

During the Great Depression, President Franklin Delano Roosevelt implemented the Work for Progress program to put Americans back to work in an ailing economy. It was during this time, in 1932, that Works Progress Administration (WPA) workers built a new highway through Kewanee. Today, the Simmons-Wright Company Store is less than twenty feet from Highway 11 and 80 in Kewanee.

When you step through the screened atrium of the Simmons-Wright Company Store, you take a leap back in time. The vintage display cases made from polished mahogany wood line the center aisle. The balcony above is lined with transom windows. A display of vintage shoes dating back to the 1940s and other antiques line the walls of the balcony. Below, a vintage National cash register is still used in the store. The winter chill is kept at bay by a potbellied wood-burning stove. Customers can buy hoop cheese, dairy products and staples as well as antiques.

A green bench on the porch of the Simmons-Wright Company Store was the favorite resting spot for Bernice Simmons. Mrs. Simmons was the owner

The view from the balcony that overlooks the Simmons-Wright Company's first floor. The store is located at 5493 Highway 11 and is less than a mile from Interstate 20 near the Mississippi-Alabama state line. *Courtesy of the author.*

and operator of Simmons-Wright Company for seventy years. She died at the age of ninety-six. Since her death, it has been reported that passing motorists have seen her sitting on the green bench. The store is located at 5493 Highway 11 and 80 near the Alabama-Mississippi state line, about seventeen miles east of Meridian.

## Mayerhoff Store
### Arundel

From the capture of Francis Albrecht Mayerhoff's the *Indian Queen* by the French to the colonial trading post near Aliceville, Alabama, the deep-rooted mercantile business in Arundel dates back over one hundred years before the doors of Mayerhoff's General Store opened.

Decades have passed since the families of German immigrant Francis Albrecht Mayerhoff petitioned the U.S. government for repayment for the *Indian Queen*, a merchant ship captured shortly before the Napoleonic Wars of 1800–15. It was during this period that pirates commandeered merchant ships. This incident is referred to in a letter penned by George Fredrick Mayerhoff:

> *When Charles Francis was four years old, his father, Francis Albrecht Mayerhoff left Düsseldorf, Germany and engaged in the merchant business in New York City. Mayerhoff lost a large amount of cotton and tobacco on his ship the "Indian Queen" before he settled at Mayerhoff Springs near Basic City in Clarke County.*

Some mention of the ship *Indian Queen* and the incident is on page forty-seven of *The French Assault on American Shipping, 1793–1813: A History and Comprehensive Record of Merchant Marine Losses* by Greg H. Williams. The book gives this detailed account of reported loss:

> *Adventure, 146-ton brig, Benjamin Bioren, master. Built at Bristol, Pennsylvania, in 1792. Abraham Piesch and Francis Mayerhoff, of*

Wood shutters cover the windows of the closed Mayerhoff Store, located on Highway 11 in Arundel, Lauderdale County. *Courtesy of the author.*

*Philadelphia, owners. Homeport Philadelphia. Left Delaware Capes for Hamburg on December 14, 1798, with cotton, sugar, logwood, deerskins, rice, coffee, and pimento. The owners owned $7,509.23 on invoice, Thomas and John Clifford owned $7,011.46, Pratt and Kintzing owned $900, John Shropp owned $811.21, and other amounts were owned by Amie Brandt and C.N. Burke and Co. Seized on January 9th by Captain Guellimein's French Privateer LeJuste, of St. Malo, and taken to Brest where Captain Bioren and his crew were imprisoned. Vessel and cargo condemned on February 19, 1799, because of the rôle d'équipage wasn't signed by a naval officer and passenger on board was not listed. Decision affirmed on appeal at Qumper. Captain Bioren was ordered to pay a fine of 50 livres.*

Although the awards are listed, no mention is made of the owner or owners of the *Indian Queen* on page 190:

Indian Queen, *ship, Captain Russell, master. Loss reported by Matthew Clarkson, Abraham Barker, Nathaniel Willis, Samuel Hammond and Josiah Richmond. An award of $72,399.15 was made under the July 4, 1831 convention with France*

Good fortune would follow when Francis and his son, Charles, migrated to Pickens County, Alabama, and opened a trading post near Aliceville in the early 1800s. Ultimately, though, the call of wandering feet led them near Enterprise, Mississippi.

Before 1900, Charles E. Mayerhoff established a sawmill at Sageville and built a railroad spur to connect with the M&O to ship lumber from his mill.

By 1906, the Mayerhoff brothers, Charles E., George and Fletcher, direct descendants of Francis, who were aided by a railroad-logging spur, were well established in the lumber business, and in that same year, they purchased the old Pachuta Lumber Mill, which became known as C.E. Mayerhoff Lumber Mill.

C.E. Mayerhoff built a company store nearby for the convenience of workers who didn't have transportation into Shubuta to purchase staples. Like many company store owners, Mayerhoff paid his employees in doogaloos instead of U.S. Treasury money. This doogaloo is a small brass token imprinted with the value and the C.E. Mayerhoff name. Most sawmills and plantation workers shopped at company stores, where the full face value of the brass token was accepted.

The C.E. Mayerhoff Lumber Mill had once been located near the old stagecoach route in Sageville, Lauderdale County. *Courtesy of Mayerhoff family archives.*

Francis Albrecht Mayerhoff's descendants still reside in Sageville, which was once a tourist destination for travelers to enjoy Arundel Springs Hotel amenities and its spring of healing mineral waters.

Although the hotel and springs have long disappeared, the railway that once transported tourists who disembarked from the hack line that lay directly across from Mayerhoff Store is there to this day.

Our imaginations can witness the arrival of the hotel carriages, and we can listen to the neigh of restless horses awaiting the train to ferry its guests away. Lively hoofbeats would mingle with the revelry of ladies dressed in an array of delicately embroidered silks and satin trimmed in lace with ruffles and beading that draped over feet clad in high-top buttoned-down shoes as they were swished away by waiting carriages to enjoy the healing waters of the springs and canoe rides. Or perhaps one could listen to chatter as the ladies strolled among the resort's shaded grounds while awaiting festivities, at which the demure eyes of the younger ladies would coyly flutter as they waltzed across the floor with an admirer.

Lucy Mayerhoff clerked the Mayerhoff General Store. Like other store owners of the time, she honored the custom of keeping credit for her

The front of this doogaloo, used to pay sawmill workers, has the owner's name, C.E. Mayerhoff, imprinted on the brass token. *Courtesy of Mayerhoff family archives.*

customers. Winters were cold in Mississippi during the early to mid-1900s, and Miss Lucy was kept warm by a potbellied coal-burning stove.

"During the 1940s, the 'Blue Goose,' a bus that ran from Meridian into Clarke County, occasionally stopped at the store to pick up or drop off a passenger," Mary Ruth Bodron said. Mary Ruth Bodron is among the memory keepers, the doorways to our past, who hand down memories to new generations to preserve the places we lived and those we loved and admired.

The Mayerhoff Store, which is no longer in business, is located on Highway 11 South, coming from Meridian.

## Dave Carr General Store
## Whynot

Whitesville, located on the Meridian-to-Mobile trading path during the early 1800s, is probably named in honor of W.H. White, an early settler, landowner and merchant who lived near Mount Horeb Baptist Church. He might have been the first general store owner in Whitesville.

Among its residents, the name Whitesville stuck until application to the U.S. Postal Service for a post office in 1852. The petition was denied since a post office existed by the same name in Mississippi.

Stories have been spun and retold about the origin of the name Whynot, and the debate continues, even today, whether it is one word or two. One often-repeated story of the name comes from when the naming committee for Whitesville reached a stalemate. In exasperation, it is said, one member stood up, threw his hands into the air and said, "Why not just call it Whynot!" Apparently, others agreed, for when the dust of the verbal battle ended, the community officially adopted the name Whynot. According to Lauderdale County tax collector Stanley Shannon, "The name of Whynot came from a village in the Carolinas." Since many of Whynot's early settlers migrated from the Carolinas, in all probability, this would be the correct assumption.

The postal service approved application for a post office in Whynot on May 5, 1876, and appointed Daniel McInnis as postmaster. Another postmaster was appointed in 1882, and Louis Kornegay became postmaster in 1893. The post office ceased its service on June 8, 1908, while James H. Clark was serving as postmaster.

The general store located in Whynot is on old Highway 19 South situated near the railroad track. The general store belonged to Dave (D.W. Sr.) Carr before Johnnie Booker opened an antique shop in the building. The general store and Booker's Antique Shop have closed.

Of course, the story of the town's name is not the only famous legend of Whynot. Eighty-seven years later, in 1963, Whynot would be the birthplace of David Ruffin, who recorded on the Motown label while he was the lead singer for the Temptations. His elder brother, Jimmy, alternated as lead singer for the group. In fact, no matter what part of the state you go to, you'll find famous writers, actors and singers from the blues to rock 'n' roll.

D.W. Carr Sr. once operated a general store in this building near the railroad track in Whynot. The store later became Johnnie Booker's antique shop until it closed. *Courtesy of the author.*

## Tom Lyle Grocery
### Meridian

Nettie Henry's father was sold to a family who removed him to Texas when Nettie was a young girl. After the war, her father walked from Texas to be reunited with his family in Meridian. He rented land from a Mr. Ragsdale, who might be Lewis A. Ragsdale. Lewis Ragsdale, along with Richard McLemore and John Ball, was one of the three founding fathers of Meridian, according to an interview by the WPA with Nettie. Nettie had been one of John C. Higgins's slaves. Higgins was a farmer and slave owner who lived on the high hill, which is probably near the present-day Rose Hill Cemetery on Eighth Street (then called Seventh Street) in Meridian before the war.

In the interview, Nettie said the Yankees carried off all the mules and horses, burned plows and destroyed the railroad tracks. According to Nettie, the Yankees burned seventy homes and all the stores; when the Yankees' pillage had ended, not even a rooster had been left behind.[23]

The railway in Meridian had been important to the Southern cause. Trains were used to transport Confederate soldiers, ammunition and other goods. In the early hours before dawn on the morning of February 19, 1863, during the height of the war, Confederate troops were aboard the train bound for Vicksburg. When the train began to cross the Chunky River Bridge west of Meridian, which had been weakened by floodwaters, the train derailed and plunged into the river below. The First Choctaw Battalion, camped nearby, was the first to arrive on the scene. Choctaw native Jack Amos, who was a member of the First Choctaw Battalion, was the first to leap into the ice-cold waters and rescue many of the drowning Confederates who survived the crash.

After the war and during Reconstruction, in 1866, a new mayor, William Sturgis, was elected. Within the year, Yankees began a form of devilment in the village and set fire to Theodore Sturgis's (the mayor's brother) large store. The mayor blamed the Ku Klux Klan and continued an effort to rid the state of the hooded Klan members. The following may be related to the incident Nettie Henry spoke of during her WPA interview.

While in court, the accused, Bill Dennis, a freed slave, pulled his pistol and fired. The acrid smell of gunpowder fill the courtroom before Dennis discovered his shot had been off. Instead of shooting his intended victim, who might have been Theodore Sturgis, he mortally wounded Judge Bramlette.[24]

Several attempts had previously been made to remove Sturgis from office without success. But after the courthouse incident, Sturgis, not of his free will, was placed on a northbound train. He had served less than one year as mayor.

Tom Lyle, a prominent and wholesale grocer after the Civil War, provided staples and farm supplies to Meridian and rural communities as the county moved into a new century. In 1906, the tornado that decimated a portion of Meridian also destroyed Tom Lyle Grocery.

Just east of Meridian, across the Alabama line in Copiah County, the gypsy king, Emil Mitchell, and his band of gypsies camped while he awaited the birth of his thirteenth child. Unfortunately, soon after his wife died during childbirth, her body was transported to Meridian, a city with adequate ice to preserve her body until gypsies could arrive from across the United States. The population of Meridian doubled as gypsies arrived to pay respects to their queen. It is said no gypsy would tell fortunes during this period for fear of bad luck. A newspaper account of the wake and funeral published in the *Meridian Dispatch* on February 1914 gave an account of the queen's

Shown is Tom Lyle Grocery Co., which may be the original store before the 1906 tornado destroyed a portion of Meridian. *Courtesy of Lauderdale County Department of Archives and History.*

wake. Her dress was that of gypsy royalty, her braids were interwoven with rare coins and, on her head, was a kerchief tied according to gypsy custom. Her children brought gifts and placed them in her casket. The youngest child affixed earrings to her mother's ears. The St. Paul Episcopal Church overflowed, and gypsy mourners gathered around the church. The king of the gypsies of North America followed his wife's horse-drawn, glass-covered hearse up Seventh Street to Rose Hill Cemetery. Over five thousand gathered at her grave. Both the king and queen of the gypsies, Emil and Kelly (Callie) Mitchell, are buried at Rose Hill Cemetery on Eight Street in Meridian.

## Marion General Store
### Marion

Marion is named for Revolutionary War hero Francis Marion, who was known as the "Swamp Fox" because his sly cunning outwitted the British during the war. Marion Station is the original county seat of Lauderdale County. The town established a post office on January 31, 1854, after Virginian Jubal B. Hancock arrived with his Choctaw wife and became postmaster.[25]

In 1846, appointed town marshal Jubal Hancock carried a stick instead of a gun. He used a stick in an attempt to end a feud between Fisher and his sons and S.S. Shumate and his wife, Muggie, over the ownership of the Marion brickyard. Hancock managed to temporarily defuse tempers.[26]

It may have been hours or days later, but the Fishers, with blood in their eyes, and perhaps whiskey in their guts and faith in the flint rock shotguns they held, eventually called Muggie Shumate and her husband out.

The wood plank door swung open, and Muggie stepped into view with two single-shot guns by her side, her husband close behind her. She dropped one to the ground and then raised the other gun and fired. Fisher dropped before his son William fired a missed shot. Muggie raised her preloaded second gun and pointed it at William. Muggie hit her mark.[27]

Muggie's husband, S.S., dropped his gun and ran. Muggie, consumed with anger over his cowardice, reached for his gun and shot him as he fled. However, she should have saved the shot for the remaining Fisher, for he stood poised and fired off his shot at Muggie, a shot that ended her life and the saga of the Marion brickyard shootout.[28]

Jubal Hancock became a man who wore many hats, and he wore them well. He became Marion Station's second postmaster when he was appointed on January 31, 1854. This postmaster position had originally been held by Lewis Smith, the first postmaster, who had been appointed on January 23, 1839.

Hancock later joined with Sylvanus Evans and practiced law. He filed a claim with the U.S. government where he furnished proof of claim for compensation for reservation land held for his wife. Hancock's claim was referred to the committee on Indian Affairs, which granted the exchange of, but not compensation for, reservation land on May 25, 1842.[29] Hancock became a judge before his death in Clarke County. His body is interred at Quitman Cemetery.

Marion Station lay in the direct path of the approaching M&O rail line in 1855. The town was chosen as the M&O flag stop, that is, until John Ball competed for the flag station in the smaller village of Sowashee. Not only did Sowashee become the railway's choice, but the village also changed its name and captured the title of county seat. On May 29, 1861, Sowashee's name changed to Meridian, the same day the first train arrived over the rails of the Southern Road, which would later be known as the Vicksburg Meridian Road.

But that was before the war, before Sherman lit his torch and burned Meridian and its Confederate arsenal and ripped up its rail lines. When Sherman and his troops left, Meridian lay in ashes. When Meridian was rebuilt, the Jewish population of Marion Station removed its congregation

This general store in Marion displays an advertisement that is probably for the Meridian Hotel. The store is now used as a fabrication shop and is located across from the railroad. *Courtesy of the author.*

to Meridian. After the war, Robert J. Mosely was appointed postmaster of Marion Station on November 6, 1866, as Meridian grew into a thriving city.

The railway brought Meridian into its prominence, and in 1887, thousands of cotton bales were brought to Meridian by ox and wagon to be shipped by rail. This traffic caused the streets of Meridian to become congested.

The New Orleans and Northeastern, a railroad company that employed approximately three hundred, needed its rails and engines to be manufactured in Meridian, a city with a strong presence in agriculture and manufacturing. The population had tripled by 1994, an increase probably directly related to its 38 percent growth in manufacturing and which also caused a need for housing.[30] Marion Station, now known as Marion, declined as Meridian's growth increased in the early 1900s. Yet Marion still has a story to tell. A faded advertisement is still visible on the side of the general store in Marion.

The store, which represents a part of Marion's history, is significant since the building appears to have been built before 1900. The building is now used as a fabrication shop on Marion Drive.

## James' Grocery and Market
### Causeyville

This country store was once located on the southeast corner of Causeyville's crossroad. Earl and Flake Ford were among the former proprietors of the general store before 1980. A Lauderdale County Health Department nurse visited the store and gave immunization injections to infants and children in the community

during the 1970s. The Fords leased the store to Wayne Raley and then James Irby, who became the last proprietor before the store was dismantled in 1987.

# WARREN COUNTY

## Buck's General Store
### Bovina

Long after exploding cannonballs lit up the night sky over Vicksburg, the Mississippi River still flowed by its banks and paddle-wheel steamboats once more passed lazily by this port city.

Gone were the large cotton plantations, and in their wake, magnificent antebellum homes fell into disrepair like the cannon-littered landscape. Changing times and customs crept in as a new era rose in the South. To be southern is to be resilient, and Vicksburg's southern gentlemen and genteel women were resilient and determined to find a new way of life after the turn of the century.

Progress did come to Vicksburg after the war and Reconstruction, and it came in the form of its citizenry. In 1934, James Buck, a local farmer, cattleman and entrepreneur, began work on his general store and gristmill located on the corner of Highway 80 and Mount Alban Road, less than four miles north of the city.

Few had the grit during the Great Depression to begin a new business, let alone a grocery store at a time when jobs and money

James' Grocery & Market was located at the intersection in Causeyville. The store was one of two that served the community until it was dismantled in 1987. *Courtesy of Doris Irby.*

were almost nonexistent. However, James Buck, embedded with the same southern resilience as his grandparents, forged ahead. James Buck and his wife, Josephine, both of African American descent, opened the first store to serve the community during a time when battery-operated radios squawked over airways and kept families in touch with the nation until electricity arrived in the rural South in the 1930s.

Hard times hit the area again during World War II, but James Buck was a resourceful man and didn't allow rationing to stop him. He raised chickens, hogs and cattle and then butchered his own farm livestock to sell in his store. "People came from miles around," said the current storeowner, Randall Mauck. "Mr. Buck didn't ration meat; he would sell them as much as they wanted to buy."

"James Buck and his wife, Josephine, fed the needy [who] came through the area. And those without transportation came by foot," Ronnie, Buck's grandson, said. "To them, it was all about people in need. They never turned anyone away."

"My grandfather James Buck was born shortly before the turn of the century in 1898. Both my grandparents inherited light skin," Ronnie said. "They could have easily passed as white." He chuckled. "My grandparents ran the store for many years," Ronnie said. "Josephine, my grandmother, was in her sixties when my grandfather passed away. Grandmother at age sixty-five followed her dream and attended college and in 1976 she received her bachelor of science degree."

"My brother and I used to dig around in the area," Ronnie laughed. "But most everything had been dug up by pregnant women eating red clay dirt. I never understood that," he said. "We could see women with brown paper bags walking, picking out clay dirt in the hill across from the store until their bag was filled." Ronnie laughed and then said, "Those women carried off an entire hill."

"I grew up in the store," Ronnie said. "Grandmother said, 'Running a store is a day-to-day job.' She allowed local people to charge purchases. When I asked her why, she told me, 'It's a good way to get repeat customers; they come into the store and pay their bill, then charge again.'"

"During the civil rights [movement], a group of vigilantes tried to set fire to the store and then fired gunshots at my grandmother Josephine Buck's house; a bullet narrowly missed one of her grandsons. This act only brought the two races closer, and they banned together," Ronnie said.

"Our store," Ronnie said, "at the time, this store was the only one for ten miles, and people of both races come to shop."

Randall Mauck, a soft-spoken man, waited on customers in the former Buck General Store and spoke of the days before his father, John, purchased the store in the 1971.

"After Vicksburg fell on July 4, 1863," Randall Mauck said, "our captured Confederate soldiers were paroled. Most of the parolees came by foot down the railroad about a mile from here and gathered in the field behind the store. After a couple of days, they dispersed in all directions."

"People sometimes come and dig behind the store looking for relics from the Civil War. We don't encourage digging," his voice lowered, as if to reveal a secret. "So we don't talk about the Civil War objects found around here."

"The original bridge crossing the Big Black River burned during the war," Randall said. "And in 1876, a newly constructed bridge replaced it. The old bridge trusses are still there, but [they are] now covered with graffiti. I guess you could say—"

A customer browsing through the store interrupted. "What is this?" he asked, pointing to a black box.

"Switch box," Randall muttered. "It's an old railroad engineer's box from the steam engine days. Someone was going to throw it away, and I asked for

Buck's General Store is a block building and was constructed by James Buck. The interior is typical of general stores built in the early 1930s. This old lantern and railroad toolbox are displayed in the store. *Courtesy of the author.*

it and brought it to the store," he said. "Still has the fellow's name on it, too." The customer held up a small rusted object and asked, "What is this?"

"Lantern," Randall, who seemed to be a man of few words, said. "A carbide lantern used by the railroad many years ago." He abruptly turned his attention to another customer.

By the time Mr. Buck established his store in 1935, Coca-Cola was sold in most stores across the country.

"When I was growing up," retired schoolteacher and Randall's mother, Johnnie Mauck, said, "like many people in the community, my brother and I bartered. We would take eggs to Mr. Buck's store and trade for ice cream." Johnnie was friends with Josephine Buck while the Bucks owned the store.

"During this time," Johnnie said, "schools and churches were separate even though both races in the community worked together and often formed close bonds of friendship."

"Grandmother Josephine Buck," Ronnie said, "added a menu during the construction of Highway 80 and sold homemade soup to the men who worked on the highway during its construction." Although the store was an important part of the Buck family's life for decades, Mrs. Buck made the decision to sell the store in 1971, after her husband passed away. And there was only one person Mrs. Buck trusted to carry on the store's tradition.

"Mr. Buck and his wife were good friends of ours," Mrs. Mauck said. "James Buck and his wife, Josephine, were thought highly of in the community."

"Many people in the area tried to buy the store," said Johnnie Mauck, "but Mrs. Buck told my husband, 'I'm going to sell the store to you, John, because I know you will take care of it.'"

"When we were small," Johnnie continued, "my brother and I often hid in the bushes on Sunday mornings near the black church and listened to the preaching and singing. We would sometimes watch the baptisms in a small pond behind the church. The pond has long since filled in, but the church remains."

John Mauck, Johnnie's husband, recalled the days of boycotts in Vicksburg. "People were posted outside a store to prevent other blacks from entering the store and making purchases. The Buck's store wasn't affected by the boycott, and many came to shop. It was during this period someone tossed a cocktail bomb at the store; arson seemed to be the motive, but little damage from the fire occurred before the flames were extinguished," John said.

## The Old Store
### Bovina

The Brabstons have a long history in Bovina that dates back before the war when William Brabston and his wife settled on a plantation in Warren County. Brabston, it is said, became a member of the Whig Party and didn't cotton much to the war for Southern states' rights.

But he wasn't the only Brabston who was political. William H. Brabston, a candidate for county supervisor, did what so many politicians had done in the past—he gathered at the precinct-polling place, awaiting election results from the precinct's polling box.

But the election day of August 24, 1889, wasn't an ordinary day at the Newman's Grove voting precinct. Instead, the day would end in murder. Jim Lanier, emboldened by too much drink, insulted and struck the supervisor candidate with a stick. This angered William H. Brabston, and he drew his pistol and fired.[31]

It remains a mystery as to why the candidate's cousin William Frederick Brabston fired a round of shots that proved to be fatal to William H. Brabston. William Frederick Brabston, who was tried twice, was never convicted for the murder of his cousin. Agnes Brabston, the widow of William H. Brabston, was forced to sell her husband's possessions.[32] One of Agnes Brabtson's descendants, Thomas Brabston, was responsible for the construction of the general store.

"Thomas Brabston operated a sawmill behind the store. He built his sawmill manager a house before he built the store," Bill Vinzant of the Old Store said. "Thomas wanted to give his sons something to do, so he built the store in 1915. Within a year, his sons began to complain to their father that the store took up too much of their time, and Thomas told them to shut it down."

"The store had been called the Ed Brabston Store," eighty-year-old Bryan Brabston said.

After Thomas Brabston's sons closed the store, its function as a general store would cease for the next seventy years, although it was rented out to farmers from time to time as a storage building for hay.

In 1922, tragedy struck Bovina when, in full view of the school and Child's General Store, an oncoming train collided with an open-air school bus, killing the driver. Several children were thrown from the open bus on impact and died.[33] Two of James and Nellie Brabston's sons were young boys the day the school bus attempted to cross the railroad track. William

Originally named the Ed Brabston General Store, this store is now known as the Old Store and operates as an antique shop. *Courtesy of the author.*

Patrick and Claude Brabston were among the lucky few who escaped with minor injuries. Not since the Civil War had such devastation caused so much heartbreak in the small community of Bovina.

"Scott Vinzant purchased the store in the late 1980s," Bill Vinzant said. Until that time, the doors of the old store had been closed for over a half century. Today, the store serves as an antique shop aptly named the Old Store. The painted walls and wide plank floors stand as a remembrance of Bovina's once prosperous Brabston family and plantation. The store is located at 6216 Warrior Trail, Vicksburg, Mississippi.

## SHARKEY COUNTY

### Onward Store
### Onward

When you arrive in Onward, you've arrived at the store built in 1913 by Bernard Pearl. It is said that Onward is the namesake of an 1800 plantation in Sharkey County. The county is the namesake of William Lewis Sharkey, who came to Mississippi in 1803 from Tennessee.[34]

After Reconstruction, martial law was lifted, and Sharkey became the provisional governor of Mississippi, appointed by President Andrew Johnson to restore order and statehood. Sharkey County had been carved from Warren and Washington Counties, as well as a large portion of Issaquena County in the 1870s.[35]

Long before Sharkey settled on the rich fertile soil of the lower Delta, Native Americans, who were mound builders, inhabited the land. The mound builders were agriculturists, hunters and fishermen who settled here thousands of years before the first settler set foot on Mississippi soil.[36]

The Mississippi Territory became a prime hunting spot for dignitaries and politicians. In 1902, to help resolve a territorial boundary dispute

Onward General Store serves lunch and a slice of American history. *Courtesy of the author.*

between Mississippi and Louisiana, as well as to have the opportunity to hunt black bear, Theodore Roosevelt boarded a train with Sharkey County as its destination.

If you could ask Theodore Roosevelt, the twenty-sixth president of the United States, he would probably tell you about his famous bear hunt near Onward. Roosevelt and his guests arrived by train on November 14, 1902, eager for a bear hunt. He mounted his horse for the two-mile trip southward to the Smedes Plantation, where he would rendezvous with Governor Andrew H. Longinos and his party. Roosevelt's guests followed his lead in wagons laden with supplies for the campsite.

Holt Collier, a former slave who served in the Confederate cavalry, a bear hunter himself, had been Roosevelt's appointed guide. Collier, it is said, cornered the exhausted bear and tied it to a willow tree to deliver on his promise of a live bear.

Theodore Roosevelt, an avid sportsman, refused to shoot a captive bear, and based on this noble act, the teddy bear was created by Rose, the wife Morris Michtom, a Jewish merchant who immigrated from Russia and sold notions in his Brooklyn, New York shop.

The interior of Ownward General Store in Sharkey County. *Courtesy of the author.*

Morris Michtom and his wife, Rose, capitalized on Roosevelt's sportsmanship in the Delta and created the popular teddy bear that had met Roosevelt's approval to carry his nickname, Teddy. The popularity of the teddy bear led to the creation of the Ideal Toy Company.[37]

While in office, Roosevelt signed a bill to protect certain lands as refuges for wildlife. This bill was a forerunner to the creation of the National Park Service during Franklin D. Roosevelt's New Deal.

Roosevelt's guide, Holt Collier, died in 1936, shortly before the great flood decimated Greenville when the Mississippi River broke its levee at Mound Landing on April 21, 1927. Holt Collier is buried at Greenville's Live Oak Cemetery.

Onward is surrounded by the flat fields of the Delta region, where the sweltering heat of summer stirs nothing more than dust. An almost extinct community left with nothing but a story to tell from a photograph-lined wall at the Onward Store.

Painted paw prints on the floor of Onward General Store are reminders of the president who once camped and hunted in the cane breaks of Sharkey County, and like the train Roosevelt arrived on, his bear hunt is nothing more than a ghost of a long-forgotten memory.

Onward Store is located north of Vicksburg at 6693 Highway 61.

# JASPER COUNTY

## R.H. Read General Store
## Paulding

It could be said that Jasper County's checkered past began when Paulding, a stagecoach route to Mobile, snubbed the railroad and ended when delegates from Paulding refused to ratify the Thirteenth Amendment. Mississippi is one of the few southern states that did not abolish slavery. However, the required three-quarters of states did ratify the amendment, and it became part of the Constitution on December 18, 1865, and slavery ended in the nation, including Mississippi.

Paulding is one of two county seats in Jasper County; the other county seat is Heidelberg. Paulding is named for Revolutionary War hero John Paulding. Its history began in 1833, when a man tried for bigamy would feel the scorch of hot iron against his cheek, branded with the letter *B* to signify his unlawful deed.

Robert John Moore sits on a bench outside R.H. Reed's General Store in Paulding. The store shows signs of age. *Courtesy of the author.*

Nearly 150 years later, there isn't much left of the bustling town once called the Queen City of the East with well-to-do citizens and entrepreneurs, like Robert H. Read, who, according to his World War I draft registration card, was born in Paulding on May 28, 1876. The general store has been an important part of life in Paulding for almost a century, and its history runs deep, as Robert John Moore would tell you. Mr. Moore has been Paulding's memory keeper for the past 87 years.

The R.H. Read General Store, built by Read before 1910, has been an important part of life in Paulding since James H. Jones acted as deputy sheriff.[38] He might have been the deputy who pursued the shooter who felled a man on a Paulding sidewalk. The shot man wrote the name of the shooter in the blood that flowed from his body, and Dr. William T. Street, the town physician, might have tried to save him.[39]

R.H. Read's store remains much as it did almost one hundred years ago. Long planks of unpainted lumber run the length of the building, and like most other general store owners in the South, Read sold everything from clothing to planting supplies. He would later add a cotton gin and build a twelve-room house, where he and his wife, Mattie, raised their children.

"Mr. and Mrs. Read were friendly people," Robert Moore said. "Mrs. Read worked in the store, too. We had to wait until the white people were waited on, and we had to wait and eat after white people, too."

This was during the time when the store proprietor or clerk filled a customer's order. Help-yourself stores had not yet made their appearance in the rural South.

"In the 1920s, a black man was charged with assault on a woman," Moore said. "They built a gallows and hanged him in front of the courthouse. Some people said he didn't do it; he was innocent."

His gaze fell in the direction where the courthouse had once been. He hesitated and then said, "This is the third courthouse in Paulding. The original burned in 1932, and the second one was pushed into a gully."

Legends can grow larger than life. However, legends often remain unproven, as in the case of a young African American woman who was sentenced to the gallows. Although details of her crime are unknown, legend says that a local doctor offered her all the gingerbread she could eat in exchange for her body after her death. The young girl accepted his offer, and she had all the gingerbread she could eat before she went to the gallows.

Robert Moore sat on a weathered, outdoor bench that sagged. He spoke softly, his humble demeanor and kindness showing through his eyes. He paused briefly and drifted back into history where a picture of Paulding emerged, the one he remembered as a young boy.

"I worked in a saw mill for ten cents an hour, a dollar a day in 1948," Moore said. "But I became a top-paid man making twenty-five cents an hour."

His voice filled with pride as he spoke. He had accomplished what some might have thought impossible for a man of color in that era.

# NESHOBA COUNTY

On land ceded by the Choctaws in 1830, Neshoba County was formed on December 23, 1833. The county name, Neshoba, comes from the Choctaw language. Its county seat of government is Philadelphia. Neshoba County is the site of a Choctaw reservation.

## Williams Brothers General Mercantile Store
### Williamsville

To experience the atmosphere of an authentic general store of a bygone era, one must visit Williams Brothers General Store in Williamsville, where slab bacon and hoop cheese reign as king. Williams Brothers is located within spitting distance of Philadelphia, Mississippi. Southerners who have a hankering for a taste of grandma's Sunday dinner can find pickled peaches, homemade cane syrup, whole smoked or fresh hams or a case of the best sweet potatoes money can buy.

A jar of blueberry preserves from Williams Brothers General Store couldn't have been sweeter for World War II veteran First Lieutenant Amzie Cooper Williams and his wife, Frances, than on the day Ole Miss superstar and New Orleans Saints quarterback Archie Manning married their daughter, Olivia, in 1971. But life would grow sweeter for the Williams when grandsons Cooper, Peyton and Eli arrived on the scene to round out their growing family.

Williams Brothers General Store was established in 1907. The general store is located in Williamsville, which joins Philadelphia in Neshoba County. *Courtesy of the author.*

Cases of sweet potatoes grown in Mississippi are sold at Williams Brothers General Store. *Courtesy of the author.*

The Williams were well known as grocers around Neshoba County and the surrounding area long before Archie Manning became their son-in-law. Williams Brothers Grocery began 105 years ago as a general mercantile store, the forerunner of the all-purpose chain stores of today, except with one difference. It sold—and still sells—homegrown produce, cane syrup and other foods that suited a southerner's palate. Whether it's slicing rind bacon or hoop cheese, the Williams family continue to do the same thing they have done for over one hundred years—provide quality general merchandise for their customers.

Philadelphia's growing pains began when the Choctaw Nation opened its first casino on its nearby reservation. As the demand for housing and services increased, so did Philadelphia, and now, the outskirts of this movement have reached Williamsville. The general store, first established by brothers Amzie and Brown Williams, opened as a general merchandise store in 1907 to serve Neshoba County farmers.

Amzie Cooper Williams, the grandson of Amzie Williams, continued in his grandfather's footsteps. The store has remained in the Williams family with each passing generation. This country store has thrived for decades. An addition to the building of a shoe department carries name-brand shoes for men, women and children. The original attached building remains much as it did one hundred years ago. The one-cash-register store has grown to four yet reserve space for the multitude of goods, groceries, fashionable clothing and shoes.

The general mercantile store is a hotspot of activity during the Christmas holiday shopping season, but you won't find an empty shelf at this well-stocked store, regardless of the season. Year-round, the friendly staff of helpful folks will greet you; it's southern hospitality at its best.

The first appointment of a postmaster in Philadelphia occurred on February 22, 1856, and was given to Robert M. Ross in the small village that surrounded the courthouse square.[40]

The Neshoba County Fair's Giant House Party, established in 1889, is an annual event that takes place in late July to the first of August. The grounds contain over six hundred cabins for the eight-day house party, where front-porch sitters offer revelers a glass of iced tea, a southern favorite enjoyed at suppertime. The pavilion is the stomping ground for national and state politicians, speech after speech and promise after promise.

The annual Choctaw fair on the reservation near Philadelphia is the location of the World Stickball Championship. This game was once played near Chunky Chitto in Newton County before the approval of the Treaty of Dancing Rabbit Creek, an attempt to remove Indian tribes from Mississippi.

The Choctaw Indians have engaged in the violent sport of stickball for hundreds of years. When they face off on a field, sixty in number, each participant holds a sixty-inch netted stick in hand, and the battle over a baseball-sized ball begins.[41] It's a duel of netted hickory sticks until the last team is defeated and the victorious side is named World Champions.

Williamsville General Store is located at 10360 Road 375 in Williamsville.

# PIKE COUNTY

Carved from Marion County, Pike County was formed on December 8, 1815, by the territorial general assembly. Pike County borders northeastern Louisiana.

C.A. Alford General Store in Progress is located on the back right side of the intersection. Court was once held on the porch of the store. *Courtesy of C.A. Alford family archives.*

## C.A. Alford General Store
### Progress

A man of great stature once lived in Progress. He was a man of uncommon worth who possessed the gift of giving, and the day he died, Progress mourned.

Progress is an unincorporated community where Claude Alford lived. He married Inez Allen at the age of twenty-two and became a general store proprietor. It is not known who the previous owners of the general store were or what years open court was held on the porch of the general store, but it is known that a sign announced the new owner, C.A. Alford. Probably the only excitement that stirred Progress is when a tower was built near the community and when an open-air justice court was held.

# CLARKE COUNTY

From free-flowing artesian wells to steamboats and the Civil War, Clarke County has a rich history. The county, formed on December 23, 1839, has played a prominent role in the timber, agriculture and manufacturing industries. The county is named for Joshua G. Clarke, the first chancellor of the state.[42] The county seat of government is Quitman, which became the site of a Confederate hospital and cemetery. Long Bell Timber opened a large company store in Quitman. This building still exists, although it is no longer associated with the timber company. The company placed a watering trough in Quitman for horses and livestock in the early 1900s. The artesian well has flowed into the trough for almost one hundred years, and it still flows today.

## *R.M. Linton Grocery*
## *Snell*

Snell is a community located in the northeastern part of Clarke County between Buckatunna and Hurricane Creek, and among its early settlers is Susan Allen, who would have been considered a spinster. Susan applied for a land patent in Snell on May 20, 1862, and within a few years of her application, she received a land patent in October 1896 for 79.28 acres.[43]

Susan erected two buildings on this property—a log home and a frame trading post, possibly the first known trading post in the northeastern section of Clarke County. "The Tuscahoma Trail ran from Enterprise through Snell and Hurricane Creek into Alabama," Stanley Shannon said. "Wagons passed through the area day and night transporting goods." Perhaps this is why Susan established a trading post on the Tuscahoma Trail.

Susan Allen sold the property on December 2, 1899, to John C. (Clem) Haney, who appeared to be a land speculator according to land transactions recorded at Clarke County's courthouse. Haney was a stocky, blue-eyed man, according to his World War I draft registration card. After the post office closed in Snell, mail was redirected to Increase in Lauderdale County. Haney gave his address as rural delivery, Increase (Causeyville) on his World War I draft registration card. His brother, Ira E. Haney, was the 1930-census taker for the Beat Four's Snell community.

John C. Haney sold the land he bought from Susan Allen to Alvin A. Mosley, who paid Haney $3,000 for the acreage. Mosley sold the property to S.W. Davidson and his wife, Maude.

"When we began to dismantle the house about 1950, we discovered the house had been originally built with logs that were hidden beneath planks of wood. At the time, it had been estimated the building was over a hundred years old," said Bobby Davidson, who had been present when the house was dismantled.

The other structure was an old store built with lumber. "A covered porch ran the width of the building that had two rooms, one for the store; the small room was for storage," Walterine Cook said. "We lived in the old store while our house was under construction," she said.

Throughout the history of general stores in the Snell and Hurricane Creek communities, it has been determined that six general stores have previously existed: those of Susan Allen, Hulett Davidson, Charley Stills, Alvin A. Mosley, Willie Cooper and Rufus Linton. Each of the stores was located on or adjoined County Road 514.

Timber companies built railroad spurs into Mississippi's virgin forest to harvest timber.
*Courtesy of Lauderdale County Department of Archives and History.*

Long Bell Timber built a railroad spur through the community and harvested timber in its virgin forest between the late 1800s and early 1900s.

In 1903, on property that had once belonged to Susan Allen, a small post office was erected to serve the community. Allen G. Buckalew became the first appointed postmaster on October 15, 1903, followed by John C. Haney on November 11, 1904; Emily J. Ford on May 9, 1905; Ira Haney in 1906; and Wiley O. Taylor on July 7, 1913. Mail was discontinued in Snell on June 30, 1915, and redirected to Joseph Grantham's General Store (Causeyville General Store) for rural delivery.

Families worked on their farms from sunup to sundown starting in the spring through late summer. The fields were plowed, planted and hoed until the last harvest of the season. During the first stings of winter, quilts were layered on cotton mattresses that rested on open coiled bedsprings. But the dormant winter months gave farmers an opportunity to socialize at the general store.

R.M. Linton's store was lit by a bare bulb that dangled from a cord attached to the ceiling and felt as dismal in the winter months as the gray sky that merged with barren fields looked.

Rufus Linton opened the door of the cast-iron wood heater and shoved a small oak log over red-hot coals and punched up the fire. The flames caught, and Rufus closed the heater's soot-covered door. Cinders and smoke passed through the thin metal jointed flue that arched and snaked out through the wall to mingle with the crisp, clean air of early morning.

Straight chairs were placed near the heater, where locals would gather to warm themselves up, talk politics and catch up on community news. It was a time when schoolchildren walked to school on muddied clay roads, when children's after-school snacks were cold biscuits with homemade syrup poured into a finger-bored hole when boys made slingshots and girls fashioned dolls from clothespins and scraps of material.

The Linton family lived next door in a frame house that seemed to dwarf the small one-room store that joined the gristmill. On the southwest corner, Rufus raised a small herd of milk cows. He hired a local boy to milk cows in the early morning and again in the late evening.

Rufus was the community's self-taught barber who possessed, some thought, a limited talent for cutting hair. On Saturday afternoon, those in need of a haircut would sit on a wood stool, and some, like Preacher Godwin, who wasn't a preacher, were prepared for a little humor before Rufus picked up his scissors. According to Preacher, on his previous trip to the barber stool, Rufus had gapped his hair and cut one side shorter than the other. Full

The R.M. Linton Grocery was once located in the Snell community in northeastern Clarke County. Linton operated a gristmill on the premises. *Courtesy of Karen Linton Scott.*

of fun, Preacher told Rufus he wanted him to cut his hair like he did last time. "Gap it on the sides and a little on top, and cut it shorter on this side."

Rufus quipped, "I can't do that!"

"Well," Preacher said, "I don't know why not; you did it last time!"

Of course, the banter caused laughter among the men gathered in the store—just the reaction for which Preacher had hoped.

Electricity was brought to Linton's Grocery and the Snell community by the Rural Electrification Administration (REA) created in May 1935 by President Franklin D. Roosevelt. Homeowners who wished to electrify their homes furnished and installed their own power pole. The oil lamp, battery-operated radio, wood cookstove and iron wash pot became a part of the past as more rural homes became electrified. With the help of the

Tennessee Valley Authority (TVA), electric stoves and refrigerators were made affordable to rural families through private utility companies. Progress had come to the community before World War II; water lines were installed in homes, and the double-hole outhouse became nothing more than a soon-forgotten memory.

With electricity, Linton's store became the gathering place to shoot fireworks on Christmas Eve, and the children who were lucky enough to have a penny during the early 1940s bought penny candy from a glass jar inside the store. Those who were luckier got an orange and a toy on Christmas morning.

During the hot and humid Mississippi summer, Rufus used a marketing ploy to benefit his bottom line when he included hand-dipped ice cream in his store. Rufus would give a dip of ice cream to a young boy and send him outside to savor his cone in front of others. The young boy created such a craving for ice cream as his tongue swirled around the cone, licking chocolate from his lips, that those with money to spend rushed in to buy a cone.

Of course, Linton's Store had competition each Thursday, when the Rolling Store came through the community. The Rolling Store bartered for chicken and eggs and sold goods for money. The rear of the covered truck lowered to the ground to allow customers access inside to shop for goods. But Rufus managed to overcome the Rolling Store's short-lived popularity, and he continued to barber and conduct his business as usual until the 1980s. Linton's Grocery once was located near the corner of County Road 514 in the Snell community of Clarke County. Linton's store was demolished in the late 1980s.

## Willie Cooper's Store
## Hurricane Creek

Before 1896, the U.S. Postal Service combined the Whynot community in Lauderdale County with Hurricane Creek in Clarke County. In 1896, the postal service placed Hurricane Creek in the northeastern corner of Clarke County and established the post office. Former postmasters in Hurricane Creek were Ollis C. Shirley, who was appointed by the postal service on December 12, 1896; followed by Charley Stills Jr., appointed on February 1, 1914; and Stephen Jellenc on July 9, 1914.[44]

Hurricane Creek's first known church is Mount Zion, established shortly before 1868. Among early church members were the Timms, Davidsons, Reynolds, Mooneys, Goughs, Boswells, Neals, Cokers and Knights.

You wouldn't expect to find a carnival at an old country store twenty-four miles from the nearest town, especially one that was a favorite weekend hangout for teenage boys. But that is exactly what happened at Willie Cooper's Store in Hurricane Creek in 1952, when a hawker arrived with a bear and pitched his tent, challenging strapping farm boys to throw the bear. When the bear's owner didn't get any takers from the young crowd, one local teenager, William "Billy" Jefferson Davidson, agreed to be the hawker and entice his peers to pay the fee for entrance to see the bear wrestling.

Without the participation of strapping young farm boys who wanted a chance to throw the bear, the show couldn't go on. But the boys refused to wrestle a bear that towered over them, even if it was muzzled, that is, until Billy proved he could throw the bear. Not to be outdone, the boys paid the wrestling fee for a chance with the bear and possible bragging rights.

Billy knew something that the other boys didn't. There's a technique to throwing a grizzly bear, which was taught to him by the owner and which Billy kept secret. After the last show, the owner pulled up his tent and loaded up his bear and the best showman he ever had—Billy.

Willie Cooper's Store was not much more than a gathering place for tobacco-chewing men spinning yarns and playing dominos while a few guitar strummers who could pick a tune sat in straight wooden chairs and entertained themselves.

The store was closed on Sunday because Willie, a churchgoing man, was the song director at Mount Zion Church. He didn't have far to travel to church, as his home was located at the fork of the road that led to nearby Mount Zion.

## Bass General Store
## Enterprise

One would need to reach back over two hundred years to know the historic past of Enterprise, to the first Jesuit mission and to the time when Enterprise had been a bustling river port town on the Chickasawhay River—long before John McRae held the seat as the first governor of Mississippi.[45]

John J. McRae sponsored a successful attempt to travel the Chickasawhay by steamboat from Lake Pontchartrain, Louisiana, to Enterprise. The steamboat *Piney Woods*, owned and navigated by Captain Thomas Woolberton, left Lake Pontchartrain in February 1842 and became the first

Bass General Store in Enterprise overlooked the Chickasawhay River. When the town flooded in 1809, people came by boat to shop at the store. *Courtesy of Willie Roberson.*

steamboat to successfully travel up Chickasawhay River to Enterprise. With a passable river trade route, Enterprise thrived.

Enterprise is a small town on the west side of the Chickasawhay River, once an important trade center in its early history. In fact, Enterprise, a pre–Civil War cotton kingdom, has several firsts, including defending its boundaries against Southern renegades.

When the war erupted, all the South fought for states' rights, except for the free state of Jones, headed by Newt Knight from Jones County. Knight and his governing body seceded from the Confederate States and formed their own military group of about one thousand men—enough to loot and terrorize. These forces were advancing toward Enterprise, a community without Confederate troops to defend itself.

But unknown to Newt Knight, Enterprise had mustered and armed its paroled Union prisoners from the Sixth Indiana Cavalry, who, under the command of former Union solider Major Eli Lilly, had been outfought and outwitted a few miles north of Athens, Tennessee. The captured Yankee prisoners were sent to Meridian, and around ninety officers were allowed to keep a sidearm. These men were eventually sent to Enterprise by rail and, it is said, roamed freely among the townspeople and enjoyed their freedom and Southern hospitality. Union major Eli Lilly proposed that Major Ward of Enterprise, who commanded a unit of six men, "organize the Union officers as a company" to guard the town against the troops from the free state of Jones until Confederate forces could arrive from Mobile.

The former Union prisoners stood guard near the bridge. It is said that the boards were loosened in case of retreat so that the bridge could be dismantled and prevent Jones's advance. Newt Jones was forced to retreat when he discovered a company of troops had indeed fortified Enterprise.

Newt Knight, born near Leaf River in Jones County in 1832, and his band of Confederate deserters fled into the piney woods, swamps and thickets in central Mississippi to avoid capture.

Knight married Serena Turner in 1858. Legend has it that Newt's interracial relationship with a woman named Rachel is widely known, and many considered the blood of Newt and Rachel's children tainted, although her race has never been proven. Some considered her a Creole, others Native American and others black. Regardless, Newt had a strong and enduring relationship with Rachel. It is said Newt merged his two separate families into one home.

In 1863, Major Amos McLemore was sent to round up the Confederate deserters. On October 5, 1863, McLemore visited the home of Amos Deason, a resident of Ellisville. When McLemore reached the home, he might have been aware that the door swung open, and he might have seen the shooter of the gun pointed directly at him. But he would not live to name his killer. Many thought Newt Knight was the triggerman who stood in the doorway. Others claim the door still swings open every night on the very hour and minute it did the night McLemore was slain.

Sherman's forces later approached Enterprise, which was a supply depot and recruitment station, and destroyed buildings and the railroad. Sherman's troops heated the rails and tied them into bow ties. After the war, Enterprise, like other growing river towns in Mississippi, struggled. But not after a steamboat sailed up the Chickasawhay River, proving it was possible to ship goods from Mobile to Enterprise. This is the history that led to Bass General Store on the Chickasawhay River at Enterprise.

Bass General Store, owned by Willie Bass, was once an imposing structure that overlooked the west bank of the Chickasawhay River near the old iron bridge that Jesse James and his Mississippi side-kick, Charlie Bowdre, crossed after spending the night at Coker's Cabin just north of Causeyville. At least, that's Alan Sellers's account told in the early 1980s.

Lawrence Buckley (pictured) managed Bass General Store for Willie Bass. *Courtesy of Willie Roberson.*

In 1853, John Dunn migrated from Alabama and settled just north of Enterprise, in Lauderdale County, where he built a waterfall and gristmill on the banks of the Chunky River that connects to the Chickasawhay. The large waterwheel lay seventy yards from the banks of the Chunky River.

Water from the river powered the gristmill that cascaded over the sixty-five-foot waterfall, known as Dunn's Falls. An erroneous report that the Stetson hat was made at Dunn's Falls has been dispelled by a letter from the Stetson Hat Company. No proof is given, but it is thought the mill was used to make supplies for Confederate forces during the war.

Although there is no mention of a general store on the premises, most gristmills in Mississippi were located near a trading post or general mercantile store; thus, Enterprise, around four miles south, might have been the closest to Dunn's Falls. John Dunn and his wife, Elizabeth, are buried at Odd Fellows Cemetery in Enterprise.

The Chickasawhay rose from its banks and flooded Enterprise in 1902, at a time when a covered wooden bridge spanned the river. People managed to shop for necessities at Bass General Store by boat during the flood.

### The Village Market
### Pachuta

I tell you this because there are those who believe that it is true, for I have listened to the firsthand accounts of those who have been witnesses. I don't doubt their sincerity or their claim, for it is their eyes, not mine, that have seen the apparition in the market.

"She appears to be in her midfifties," Johnny Hunter said. "She wears a bonnet and a long skirt. My wife, Sylvia, and I have seen her on the balcony. Sometimes, she appears on the stairwell landing. I see her just long enough to be certain what my eyes have witnessed," he said. "We don't know who she is, so we call her 'Little Woman.'"

Although the spirit's identity or cause of demise is unknown, we can assume she died before 1912, since the hemline of women's clothing began to inch up after that year.

James Martin Adams became the merchant of a general merchandise store in Pachuta as early as 1920, and this store is now named the Village Market. Martin married Florence Gilbert in 1922. It is plausible to believe that James Martin Adams is probably the second owner of the general store. The store was once known as Adams Store, according to Johnny Hunter.

A view of the interior of the Village Market from the balcony. *Courtesy of the author.*

The Village Market is a landmark in Pachuta, a small village that thrived when turpentine and sawmills were located in the area. *Courtesy of the author.*

During the Depression, in the early 1930s, the WPA readied a dirt road for pavement. This road is known as Highway 11. Apparently, in the name of highway progress, the store had been moved to its new location directly across the road. Oxen and mules rolled the general mercantile store over logs until it reached the other side of the road at the former location of Pachuta's bank, which had burned.[46]

The store has changed ownership in the remaining seven decades. Other proprietors were Edgar Parker Hardy and Danny Hardy, who owned the store until James Skidmore became the owner and renamed it the Market Basket. Tully Lewis took possession of the store in 1961. He slaughtered and sold meat in the store's meat market.[47]

A tribe of Choctaws once inhabited the area and named the village Pachuta, named for a nearby creek.. Established in 1882, Pachuta's growth in the late 1800s and early 1900s is directly related to the railroad, timber and turpentine industries. Businesses were the Pachuta Drugstore, the Turpentine Still, the brick building of the Bank of Pachuta, a hotel that looked similar to a two-story farmhouse, the J.H. Abney General Store, the Climax Drugstore on the corner of Highway 11 and 18 and the Pachuta Telegraph and Depot.

The Village Market is located at 15479 Highway 11 in Pachuta. The store is under the ownership of Johnny Hunter as a general store and restaurant.

## Becton's General Store
## Carmichael

In rural communities, other than church and Sunday dinners, the general store was the meeting place to socialize. Among these rural stores is Becton's General Store in the Carmichael community. This store has served the community for over one hundred years.

The first postmaster of record is Archibald Carmichael, who was appointed on March 26, 1887.[48] Vida A. Keeton, the former proprietor of Becton General Store, which included the post office, served as postmistress from September 26, 1918, until her retirement on February 29, 1956.

Among the socializers at the store were the whittlers who occupied the loafer's bench. They swapped tales, and often, a whittler's knife would find the edge of the bench.

"Vida Agnes Keeton solved this problem by running a thin wire along the edge of the seat," former storeowner Frances Becton said.

The old country store became an important part of the social structure in rural communities. People in the community often gathered around the

Becton's General Store in Carmichael has served the community for over one hundred years. *Courtesy of the author.*

potbellied stove, and socializers talked politics, gave personal opinions and discussed local news.

"Lige Keeton, the merchant of record and the husband of Vida Agnes Keeton, owned most of the farm property around Carmichael. His wife, Vida Agnes, a tall, pretty woman with light brown hair worn pinned up, became the store clerk and postmaster," Francis Becton said. A narrow slot in the outside wall is a reminder that the store once served as the post office for the Carmichael community.

In the first quarter of the 1900s, Carmichael school, probably like many other rural schools across the state, formed a Girls' Tomato Club, which was the forerunner of the Home Demonstration Club for women. Tomato Clubs were organized to reach into the kitchens of rural farms in order to promote modern practices of food preservation during a time when few rural communities had electricity or plumbing. In 1911, the first Tomato Club formed in Lincoln and Copiah Counties, where soil was considered ideal for tomato plants. The club cultivated the fertile minds of young middle-class girls who were taught how to plant, preserve and market tomatoes they grew on the family farm. In 1913, the Girls' Tomato Clubs fell under a new banner of agriculture—the 4-H Club.[49]

A walkway connects Becton's General Store to the original store in Carmichael. The building still holds old farm implements and tools, and a kerosene tank is among the items once used. *Courtesy of the author.*

The interior of Becton's General Store is now used as storage. *Courtesy of the author.*

Carmichael thrived; its school, churches and people who lived off the land and worshiped one God relied on their deep faith when Hitler rose to power in Germany and World War II erupted. Carmichael, like many other rural communities in Mississippi, sent its sons to war.

Vida Agnes Keeton's ledger book from 1937 lists the names and cost of goods sold to customers. A pencil sold for $0.01, two large metal scoops of washing powder for $0.16, a pair of overalls for $1.50 and shoes for $1.95. Of course, a bottle of Coca-Cola sold for a nickel. A boiler (pot) cost $0.30, and a loaf of bread cost $0.10. Kerosene cost $0.15, and gasoline cost $0.22 a gallon. Based on an average annual income of less than $1,500 in 1937, the cost of goods sold is comparable to the wages earned today. The store also sold lard, cheese, sacks of flour and coffee, clothing, shoes and farm supplies.

"My uncle, Mack Tew, visited the store three times a day," Frances Becton said. "He was an outgoing man [who] teased Mrs. Keeton. Although she was all business, she had a sense of humor."

"We bought the store and house from the Keetons," Frances said. "But the two-story house was hard to heat, so my husband built another house for us to live in."

George Becton, a logging contractor, also served as supervisor for eight years in Clarke County. Carmichael's Becton General Store closed its doors in 2000, and with them closed a part of history.

The old general store is located at the intersection of County Road 610 and 630 in the Carmichael community of Clarke County.

# WILKINSON COUNTY

Founded in 1802, the county was name for U.S. Army general James Wilkinson. Woodville is the county seat of government and home of the *Woodville Republican*, a newspaper founded in 1824.

## Pond Store
### Woodville

Early pioneers in the Mississippi Territory traveled Native American trails that led to rivers, creeks and streams for trade. These waterways, named by the Chatas (later known as the Choctaws), held a specific meaning that described the river or the bounty along its banks.

It is one of these Chata trails that led to a watering hole for oxen and mules laden with wagonloads of cotton bound for Fort Adams. This watering hole is known as Pond, located three and a half miles from Fort Adams and fourteen miles southwest of Woodville's thriving plantations and Jewish population of merchants. Military troops were stationed at Fort Adams until 1807. The fort was located on an elevated plateau and named in honor of the second president of the United States, John Adams.

Immigrants were attracted to Wilkinson County, and many became prosperous tobacco and cotton growers.[50]

Although many German immigrants were enticed by free land in America, it is not known why two nineteen-year-old brothers, Berthold and Carl Lohmann, booked indirect passage on the ship *William Penn* that set sail from Havre, France, to London, England. The two Jewish Bavarian immigrants arrived in New York on May 4, 1866, and settled at Fort Adams, Mississippi.[51] Imagine the excitement the brothers must have felt when they arrived on the shores of America and the hardships they encountered on the long journey overland to Fort Adams.

North of Fort Adams, Berthold and Carl erected a trading post near a watering hole frequented by drivers with oxen or mules hauling wagonloads of cotton. But in 1881, fire destroyed the structure. The following year, in 1882, the brothers built the present-day Pond Store in Wilkinson County, a short distance south of Woodville.

Pond Store, built in 1881, is located in Wilkerson County and is one of Mississippi's oldest remaining general stores. *Courtesy of author.*

Among the plantations in Wilkinson County is Coldsprings. There is a local story that the Lohmanns most likely heard of a young woman who was struck by lightning while gazing out her bedroom window at the Coldsprings plantation. The legend is that her image still appears etched in the window's glass.

"By 1913, the store transferred ownership to Julian Lemkowitz, a Russian immigrant who escaped St. Petersburg, Russia, in 1882 with his young wife, Emma Sandburg, his former student," Liz Chaffin, the Pond Store owner, said. A tombstone inscription indicates he was born in Kiev, Ukraine. Perhaps before Julian left Russia, he had secured the position of newspaper editor of the *Natchez News*. He was an educated man who "spoke eight languages," according to Chaffin.

After Lemkowitz purchased the store at Pond, he applied for appointment as postmaster. The government granted his application on December 19, 1916. The post office sign still hangs over the clerk's window.

In 1920, George M. Curry, a boarder in the Lemkowitz home, worked as a clerk in the store, aided by J.H. Jolla, an African American store porter.

During Pond Store's 131-year history, the interior has remained unchanged. Rich, polished wood and glass cabinets that once displayed merchandise from the 1800s, wide plank walls and foot-worn floors that had been tread for over a century adjoin the rear living quarters of the proprietor. But the adjoining walls hold a secret.

Perhaps, you can imagine the morning Julian stepped inside the store. His jaw might have clenched and his eyes narrowed, face flushed red with a flared temper, when he discovered another robbery had occurred while he slept. He may have purposely walked toward the rear wall of the store that adjoined his bedroom wall and devised a plan.

Lemkowitz removed a plank of wood from the interior wall before he hewed out a small square that adjoined the store.

Using an adjoining portion of the store's interior and exterior wall, Lemkowitz fashioned a box. When he had finished, he placed his pistol inside the small box and slid it into the opening. Only on close inspection could the eye notice the wall had been tampered with. On a moonlit night, the box slid from the wall of his bedroom and gave Lemkowitz an eye-level unobstructed view of the store's interior. Only the proprietor knew that he aimed his pistol through the hole, until he fired a warning shot during an attempted robbery.

This ingenious plan must have ended the robbery attempts.

The Pond Store is located near the infamous Angola Prison, which was established in the late 1800s. This prison rented out convicts as farm labor.

Visitors enjoy the historic atmosphere of the Pond Store. The post office sign and cage still exist, although the store no longer functions as a post office. *Courtesy of the author.*

Angola prisoners considered this practice convict slavery. Both the store and prison are located in proximity to Pond near the Mississippi-Louisiana state line. The Pond Store is thirteen miles south of Woodville on the Woodville Pond and Fort Adams Road. The county is named in honor of Colonel James Wilkerson, who, along with Governor Claiborne, was in attendance at the New Orleans ceremony when France officially handed over the territory in the Louisiana Purchase of 800,000 acres of land that included the major port city of New Orleans.

Before the Civil War, the young Jefferson Davis lived at Rosemont in Wilkinson County. On November 6, 1861, he became the only person to hold the seat as president of the Confederacy.

When the county began to prosper with cotton plantations, it presented a need for modern transportation. Edward McGehee, a Woodville businessman, is credited with establishing the West Felicia Railroad in 1831. The railroad was used to transport cotton and timber for shipment by steamboat on the Mississippi River.

The town thrived for almost one hundred years, aided by Jewish merchants until the 1920s, when the boll weevil infested Wilkinson County's cotton crop. The cotton yield plummeted after the boll weevil sapped nutrients from the cotton plants. This was followed by the stock market crash on Black Tuesday, October 29, 1929.

A community's success is related to the prosperity of its inhabitants, but history does not tell us if the Great Depression dealt the same blow to rural general mercantile stores, since a bartering system had long been established. For 131 years, people have stepped across the threshold of the Pond Store; footsteps have polished the thick-planked floor. They have stood, perhaps like your great-grandparents, in front of a timeworn counter or gazed through the window of the post office, longing for a letter from a son or daughter, a mother or father.

The Pond Store has withstood the test of time; from the days of mules and wagons, it remains locked in the past as one of Mississippi's oldest rural general stores.

Wilkinson County has many local legends that have been passed down for generations, and the Gold Hole, a site of buried treasure, is one of these. The legend goes that bandits, chased by a posse, dug into the soft loam in Wilkinson County to hide stolen gold. Perhaps the gold was stolen from a bank or an overland stagecoach. When the bandits—possibly members of one of the most feared gangs in the Natchez district, the James Copeland gang—returned to retrieve the stolen gold, it could not be found. Although the ground was stable when the bandits buried the treasure, once the rains fell, the sandy loom turned to quicksand, and the chest sank from sight.

Over the years, attempts have been made to retrieve the gold. The last led to great disappointment when the chain that raised the chest broke and descended beneath quicksand into a lost grave. The Gold Hole, as it has become known, is located on private property.

The Pond Store is located at 182 Fort Adams Pond Road on the outskirts of Woodville. The store is steps away from a seven-hundred-acre state park and Clark Creek Nature Trail that leads to a strenuous hike through deciduous and hardwood trees that overlook scenic waterfalls and bluffs.

# HINDS COUNTY

Hinds County was formed on February 12, 1821, from Choctaw land. The county is named for General Thomas Hinds. The county holds the state capital, Jackson, chosen for its central location in the state and named in honor of General Andrew Jackson. [52]

## Harris Carmichael General Store
### Bear Creek

Travelers can still find the old country stores of an earlier era scattered across Mississippi's rural communities, although many have long closed their doors and are now nothing more than decayed relics of the past. Of the few that survived after the 1950s, many were nothing more than a meager living for their owners. But Harris Carmichael and his wife, Marian, made more than a meager living from Harris Carmichael Country Store, which is located seven miles from Utica. The Carmichaels managed to build a home next door and raise their family.

The walls of the old 1898 general store founded by W.D. Carmichael are lined with products once sold to its customers. A vintage wood-and-iron telephone is attached to the wall. A receiver, hung from a hook on the side, waits to be lifted to the ear for a voice to announce, "Harris Carmichael General Store."

Among the tables and glass cases in the store, an advertising sign on an open case that once held pants made in Mayfield, Kentucky, and signs announcing Ballbriggan shirts and Delta work shoes speak of the store's former days. A forgotten stack of dust-covered wood picture frames, intricately designed, lie on a shelf. A horse saddle, tossed across a sawhorse, sits in the midst of the aged wood floor, ceiling and walls, darkened by time.

Above the round, sagging doorknobs, sunlight drifts through the half-glassed double doors on the front exterior. Ms. Marian can only be described as exhibiting the soft-spoken, southern politeness of Melanie from *Gone with the Wind*.[53]

Harris Carmichael General Store is located at 19987 Highway 27 North. However, the store is officially closed.

Harris Carmichael, a farmer, merchant and active church member, died in 2005. His tombstone is etched with an image of the store.

## H.D. Gibbes & Sons General Store
### Learned

You don't just happen to be on the corner of Pine and Main Streets in Learned; it's a destination, a doorway to the historic community that depicts the late 1800s with nothing to distract your attention except the waft of sizzling steaks at H.D. Gibbes & Sons General Store and Restaurant. The

H.D. Gibbes & Sons General Store is reminiscent of days gone by when the country store was an important part of the community. *Courtesy of the author.*

H.D. Gibbes & Sons General Store is transformed into a restaurant on weekends, when the owner, Chip Gibbes, serves up sizzling steaks in the small community of Learned. *Courtesy of the author.*

quaint street of homes and storefronts could be from old New England or western towns portrayed in movies, less the wooden sidewalks; but Learned, in its quaintness, is purely southern.

On May 12, 1863, Yankee cannons bombarded Raymond, and the sounds of war ricocheted throughout the state. The war ended after the fall of Vicksburg on July 4, 1865, a failed attempt, some have said, for Southern states' rights.

Twenty-nine years after General James McPherson and his Union forces attacked Raymond, the United Methodist Church established its presence on Lowry Street in Learned. In that same year, 1892, H.D. Gibbes & Sons General Store opened its doors on the corner of Pine and Main Streets in Learned. The store has remained under the ownership of the Gibbes family. The current proprietor is Chip Gibbes. On Thursday nights, the store is transformed into a restaurant, and tables are arranged in the center section of the store, complete with a menu of steaks and fried chicken, a southern favorite.

Memories of days from long ago, when mothers shed tears for sons gone to war, seem to linger on this street. H.D. Gibbes & Sons General Store is among those memories that swirl on the street like fallen leaves in autumn.

# LEFLORE COUNTY

Leflore County is named for Greenwood Leflore, the son of a French Canadian, Louis Leflur, who married the niece of a Choctaw chief, Pushmataha. Leflore became the Choctaw chief of the western district in 1826.[54] His formal education came while he lived in Tennessee, after which he became a wealthy landowner. He built Malmaison, his plantation home. He furnished his mansion with imports from France. He signed the Treaty of Dancing Rabbit Creek, which led to his removal as a Choctaw chief.

## *Bryant's Grocery and Meat Market*
## *Money*

Some places are not what they appear to be, and Money, Mississippi, is one. Given the name, you would expect wealth, but instead, you'll find only two

The crumbling remains of Bryant's Grocery and Meat Market in Money. *Courtesy of the author*.

abandoned stores, a cotton gin, a church and a church parsonage broiling under the hot Delta sun.

August is hot in the Mississippi Delta, but it would become hotter in Money by nightfall on August 24, 1955. By the time the Delta sun rose over Bryant's Grocery and Meat Market, it would cast an ice-cold chill of doom.

Money would become notorious, and for good reason. Money is the location of the brutal murder of a five-foot-six stocky fourteen-year-old African American boy from Chicago.[55]

Emmett Till's mother had warned him before he boarded a bus for Money that customs were different down south. But Emmett couldn't conceive of a culture so different, and on August 24, 1955, he and two other boys walked into Bryant's Grocery and Meat Market expecting no more than a few minutes' diversion. It was a day that would never be forgotten in Money, and perhaps it is this day that caused Bryant's Grocery and Meat Market's demise.

Emmett Till stuttered; others say that he liked to brag to his friends he had a white girlfriend in Chicago.[56] No one really knows if Emmett stuttered while he was inside Bryant's Meat Market or if he was showing out for his young friends. Regardless, the owner's wife, Carolyn Bryant—a five-foot-two, 102-pound young mother who worked alone in the store—was frightened by

Till's remarks and demeanor.[57] Till, a large boy for his age, weighed 150 pounds. He probably appeared to be an adult to Carolyn.

Emmett didn't know it at the time, but what he thought to be simple, harmless mischief sealed his death warrant. He would be brutally murdered before the sun peeked over the Delta sky on August 29.

On August 28, Roy Bryant, the husband of Carolyn, and his half-brother, J.W. Milam, knocked on the door of Till's great-uncle Mose Wright, with whom Emmett was staying.[58]

Bryant and Milam forced young Emmett Till into their truck and drove away. Bryant and Milam were later arrested by the Leflore County Sherriff Department before the nude and brutalized body of Emmett Till was recovered from the Tallahatchie River on August 31. Bryant and Milam were charged with Till's murder, which became the springboard of the civil rights movement in Mississippi. Bryant and Milam were acquitted of Till's murder. They agreed to an interview with William Bradford Huie. The article "The Shocking Story of Approved Killings in Mississippi," written by Huie, appeared in *Look Magazine* in January 1955. In the article, both Bryant and Milam confessed to the murder they had been acquitted of in Sumner, the county seat of Tallahatchie County. Both men are now deceased.[59]

Till's mother arranged for his funeral in Chicago. She had given him his deceased father's ring before he departed for Mississippi.[60]

One can understand Carolyn Bryant's fear of Till's unwelcomed advances, regardless of race, but one cannot understand the brutal murder that followed.

Money is located 10.8 miles north of Greenwood on County Road 518.

## Tallahatchie Flats Commissary
## Tallahatchie Flats

Plantations flourished before the war, but after the war and the end of slavery, farm labor was replaced with sharecroppers, who were bound to the landowner. In fact, some sharecroppers were paid in tokens redeemable only at the plantation's commissary, a store owned by the plantation. The sharecroppers, both black and white, lived a life of poverty under the sharecropping system.

There wasn't much of a gulf between the lives of former slaves and that of sharecroppers, who lived meager existences after the war in sharecropping cabins on plantations and small farms in rural Mississippi. The farmer paid

Tallahatchie Flats rents sharecropper cabins (pictured) to visitors. The cabins, store and commissary were moved to this location from other plantations. *Courtesy of the author.*

for seed and fertilizer used by the sharecropper that would be deducted from the sharecropper's "share" of the profit after harvest, as well as his account at the plantation's commissary, an account that helped feed and clothe the sharecropper's family. This system prevented the sharecropper from pocketing any profits.

If you're looking to experience a day in the life of a sharecropper, Tallahatchie Flats rents sharecroppers' cabins, complete with outhouse, farm implements and a cotton patch. But make sure to come on a Saturday night so you can enjoy a good old-fashioned hoedown in the former commissary building. Tallahatchie Flats is located 4.8 miles north of Greenwood on County Road 518.

# JEFFERSON COUNTY

Jefferson County, established on January 11, 1802, is named for Thomas Jefferson. Many of the first settlers arrived before the formation of the county, and many of those settlers were of Scots-Irish heritage. It is said that within the boundaries of the county lived the notorious highwayman Samuel Mason, a bandit who plied his unscrupulous trade on unsuspecting travelers in the wilderness.

## Wagner's General Store
### Church Hill

Church Hill, a small hamlet located three miles through the cane breaks to the banks of the Mississippi River, was settled by Scots from the Tidewater region of Virginia in the late 1700s.[61]

Today, there isn't much in Church Hill except tombstones, a church, the remains of Wagner's General Store and secluded plantation homes that cling to the memories of the Scots who built southern mansions in the wilderness during the days of cotton and slavery, when plantation homes and cotton fields spoke of a man's wealth, a time when highwaymen rode through the wilderness and caused the heart of the weary traveler to quiver. The Scotsmen had fled the Tidewater district in the East and settled in what was known then as the old Maryland Settlement,[62] which later became known as

Christ Presbyterian Church, built in 1858. The church overlooks Wagner's General Store, located on Highway 553 and Church Hill Road. *Courtesy of the author.*

Church Hill. Here in the 1800s, the virgin forest spread a sheltered canopy over the rich, untouched soil, and black bears and other wildlife flourished on a bounty of food from the woodland and drink from small streams that crisscrossed the young territory.

And it was during the early 1800s, on a spring day, that Francis Baker concluded his business and prepared to leave Natchez. Baker probably rose early for his return trip to Church Hill. The rain from the night before left puddles along his path back home. Perhaps Baker's horse knew what lay ahead, for it neither neighed nor snorted; it moved quietly, slowly and cautiously through the wilderness, as if it knew the journey would lead to what its owner feared most. The horse could sense danger, even before its path was blocked, even before the highwaymen led it away, leaving Baker alone in the wilderness, as if his life meant no more than a single drop of rain.

Baker did not move. The place where fear had gripped him now filled with anger as he watched the Mason gang ride away with his supplies. He

Wagner's General Store, built about 1834, is the oldest general store in the state. The store, which once included a post office, is directly across from Christ Church. *Courtesy of the author.*

waited until the sight of the gang faded in the distance and then walked northward through the forest toward Church Hill.

This was the second time Baker had been robbed in the wilderness, but unlike the previous year, this time he could identify the men in court as members of the most notorious highwaymen in the territory: the Mason gang.

Baker's robbery occurred during an era when river pirates preyed on flatboats that drifted down the Mississippi River with agricultural products, furs and pelts. These boatmen, too, faced attacks by marauders—river pirates and Indians in hewed-out log canoes. In the late 1700s and early 1800s, the Mississippi Territory was sparsely populated.[63] Yet many in the territory, including the Indians and slaves, fell victim to yellow fever and other infectious diseases brought by the Europeans.

The first steamboat on the Mississippi River to pass Church Hill was the *New Orleans*, built by the Fulton Company located in New Orleans. It made its journey in 1811, the same year of the New Madrid earthquake. The river buckled and heaved up sunken logs. The turbulence caused by the earthquake created great difficulty for flatboats and the *New Orleans*, which had been caught in the river's upheaval.[64]

Wagner's General Store, which housed the post office, had been established around 1837. The store lies directly across from the 1858 Gothic Revival–style Christ Episcopal Church. The original log church, built on Fairchild's Creek in 1790, became the first Episcopalian church in the state.

General stores often acted as a repository for local news and offered warnings as well as greetings. Surely, men would have discussed the highwaymen at the general store in the Scots' old Maryland Settlement—especially men who feared the gang of bandits who trailed unsuspecting traders in the wilderness.

## Alston's Grocery
### Rodney

A common bond lies between the moss-strewn oaks of the hamlet of Rodney and Caesar Rodney, who was a signer of the Declaration of Independence. It is named in honor of his brother, Judge Thomas Rodney, the chief justice of the Mississippi Territory. The good citizens of Petite Gulf, a settlement named by the French in 1763, changed the village's name to Rodney in 1829.

Rodney's Presbyterian congregation met on Sunday morning at a local barroom until 1832. During this year, the Rodney Presbyterian Church, which had been pastored by Jeremiah Chamberlin, a missionary from

This brick church in Rodney still bears the scars from the Union boat *The Rattler*, which shelled the church with cannonballs during the Civil War. *Courtesy of the National Archives.*

Pennsylvania, was completed. It is said the bell tower held a bell cast from parishioners' silver dollar donations.

In August 1843, an outbreak of yellow fever took its toll on Rodney's residents, and deaths from the disease were so numerous that the hammer of the coffin maker rang out day and night.[65]

Before the war, Virginia native Dr. Haller Nutt settled in Rodney. He became one of Mississippi's most successful plantation owners from his invention of a new strain of cottonseed that greatly out-produced previous strains. Dr. Nutt, an innovator and entrepreneur of his day, also made improvements to Eli Whitney's cotton gin by adding steam power. With these two improvements, Mississippi became the land of King Cotton.

Dr. Nutt's octagon-shaped plantation home, Longwood, has also been called Nutt's Folly, partly because he began construction on his six-story home near Natchez shortly before the outbreak of the war. During the war, Union forces attempted to blockade the South's shipment of supplies. Blockades were placed on the Mississippi River, a main artery of shipment, and prevented the completion of Dr. Nutt's home before his death.

Zackary Taylor, whose Cypress Grove plantation home is near Rodney, was elected president of the United States in 1848.[66] Within twenty-three years, the man who eloped with Taylor's eighteen-year-old daughter would become the only president of the Confederacy—Jefferson Davis. Davis's young bride, Sarah Knox Taylor Davis, died within three months of her marriage.

On April 12, 1860, the first gunshot at Fort Sumter, South Carolina, began a battle that divided a nation. Within four months, from December 1860 to March 1861, eleven Southern states had succeeded from the Union. The war left the South in the ashes of its failed attempt for independence. Many in the South considered it a rich man's war, paid for by the bloodshed of sons, husbands and brothers.

On September 12, 1863, Union sailors attended the Presbyterian Church at Rodney. They were caught off guard, unaware of the outdoor activity until Confederate lieutenant Allen entered the church. When the lieutenant announced that the Confederate army had surrounded the church, bedlam broke out. The sailors and parishioners scrambled for cover as gunfire erupted from Confederate muskets. The hail of gunshots alerted the Federal boat *The Rattler*, whose crew fired its cannon. The church still bears the scars of this skirmish, which left a cannonball lodged in the brick arch of the center window.

In the early 1800s, the notorious land pirate John A. Murrell and his gang whipped through the Mississippi Territory. Murrell, considered the most dangerous and feared river pirate and highwayman in the Natchez district, was a charismatic and eloquent speaker who often portrayed himself as a circuit-riding preacher. Legend has it that Merrell could work a congregation into a frenzy of praise that allowed his gang to steal the congregation's horses.

Some have claimed Murrell controlled over 2,500 Mississippi River pirates and killed over 400 men, and it is told that John Murrell's scheming and persuasiveness often led to misfortune for those who encountered him.

Supposedly, Island 37 near Tiptonville, Tennessee, became Merrell's hideout, a haven on the Mississippi River created by the 1811 New Madrid earthquake. (It is also claimed that his hideout was in Missouri at Cave in the Rock.) While at his hideout, Merrell could claim citizenship in either state that faced the island—Arkansas or Mississippi. Depending on which side captured him, he could claim residence in the other state and thus be released.

Alston's General Store in Rodney in the early 1930s, long after the Mississippi River changed its course and moved five miles away from Rodney, which had been a bustling river port town in the 1800s. *Courtesy of the National Archives.*

COUNTRY STORES OF MISSISSIPPI

Merrell was eventually captured in 1834 and sentenced to ten years' hard labor in Nashville, Tennessee. He died nine months after his release from prison. He acknowledged on his deathbed that he was guilty of the charges brought against him, but he claimed that he had never committed murder. This occurred long before Alston's Grocery opened its doors in Rodney, but it's a sure bet that the story of John Murrell was told again and again by old-timers who sat on the store's loafer's bench.

Alston's Grocery had once been a flourishing business, even after the Mississippi River drifted away from Rodney's riverbank in the early 1870s. But by the mid-1940s, the population of Rodney decreased again and led to the closure of the general store. What remains of Alston's Grocery is located on a sandy lane near a green-domed church. Rodney is located off the Natchez Trace, eighteen miles north on Highway 553 in Jefferson County.

## Cohn Bro's General Mercantile
### Lorman

What led Heiman Cohn and his brother Joseph to flee Alsace, France, in 1872 is not known with certainty, but in the turbulent 1860s, France, hungry for world prominence, began to fortify its forces in preparation for war with Prussia.

Heiman Cohn arrived in Rodney, a thriving river port town before the Mississippi River receded and moved five miles west. He clerked for a merchant in Rodney until he and his brother Joseph garnered enough funds to open a general mercantile store in Clifton.

Lorman, once called Hayes City, is less than two miles from the Natchez Trace and is the location of a plantation that once belonged to a man named George P. Farley. In 1872, Charlotte, the daughter of George Porterfield, sold a portion of her inherited land to the Cohn brothers: Lehman, Heiman and Joseph. In 1890, the three brothers established the present-day store and cotton gin in Lorman.

Before the railroad came through Lorman around 1884, when Heiman worked for a merchant in Rodney, merchandise came overland from Rodney Landing on the Mississippi River.[67]

An advertisement for Cohn Bro's General Mercantile in Lorman appeared in the *Fayette Chronicle* on July 29, 1914, and listed lumber, dry goods, clothing, furnishings, hats, crockery, hardware, stoves, buggies, wagons and groceries.

Heiman Cohn died in 1903, and Lehman Cohn died in 1914. The store remained in the family until the late 1900s.[68]

Cohn Bro's General Store, built by Hiemann Cohn and his brother, is located in Lorman. The former general store is now known as the Old Country Store. The crisp white linens cover tables that are centered in the store, which now does business as a restaurant. *Courtesy of the author.*

Shelves and bins built by skilled craftsmen line the length of both walls in Cohn Bro's General Store. A ladder is still attached to a rod that runs the length of the shelves to give easy access for retrieving a customer's order. *Courtesy of the author.*

On the 1920 federal census, Daniel Cohn is listed as a merchant at a general store, and his birthplace is given as France. He lived with his wife, Rose, and their son, Heiman, who had been born in February 1919 in Mississippi.[69] The store remained in the Cohn family until 1995.

Today, Cohn Bro's General Mercantile serves as a local restaurant near the Natchez Trace. The building, now known as the Old Country Store, is located at 18801 Highway 61, north of Natchez.

# KEMPER COUNTY

Kemper County, named for Colonel Ruben Kemper, was formed on December 23, 1833, from land ceded by the Choctaws. The county, located on the eastern border of the state, is adjacent to Pickens County, Alabama.

## W.F. Rodgers General Store
### Porterville

The W.F. Rodgers General Store is located across the street from the railroad in Kemper County, a county known once known as "Bloody Kemper" for

The W.F. Rodgers General Store was once a hub of activity when the community thrived in the early 1900s. *Courtesy of the author.*

This unnamed general store with aged gas pumps and peeling paint is next to the W.F. Rodgers General Store. *Courtesy of the author.*

the murders, stabbings, hangings, shootings and lawlessness that prevailed throughout the mid-1800s to the early 1900s.

In 1913, W.F. Rodgers built the Porterville General Store,[70] and by 1930, Jack McElvaine, at age twenty-eight, had become the store's merchant.[71] Jack Webb Jr. worked as a collector for a funeral home in 1940. He may have been the Jack Webb who became the merchant after McElvaine.

Aided by the railroad, Porterville merchants and farmers prospered during the early 1900s. The town declined when farmers sought public work in larger towns. Both general stores are now closed.

## Sciples General Store
### Dekalb

As long as the water flows and the grinding stone turns, there will be fine ground cornmeal and grits for sale at Sciples Water Mill. The water mill, built in 1790 on the banks of Running Tiger Creek, has continued its operation by the Sciples family for the past 140 years.

Sciples Water Mill has been in operation since 1790 in Kemper County. The mill still grinds corn into meal and grits. *Courtesy of the author.*

More than a grinding stone was at work in Kemper County in the 1800s. Lawlessness was rampant, and the horrors of ruthless murders were reported as far west as Birmingham. Headlines were of the results: murder, brutality and poison.

In fact, a man taking a drink of whiskey offered by Dr. William Lipscomb was tempting fate, one that resulted in death by poisoning. Of course, it wasn't a random act but had been prepared before the dastardly act was carried out, and it was done in the name of life insurance benefits, a scam conceived in the deviant minds of heartless men.

Near Dekalb, after a first attempt to assassinate John W. Gully on December 19, 1876, was unsuccessful, the would-be assassin didn't lose his determination. On April 26 of the following year, his second attempt succeeded.

The lifeless body of John W. Gully was found less than a quarter of a mile from his home in Dekalb. Gully had been shot through the neck, his boots, hat and wallet taken by the murderer.[72] What led police to suspecting two men of the crime is unknown, but the following Sunday, W.W. Chisolms and H.A. Hopper were taken into custody, and a warrant was issued for two more suspects, J.P. Gilmer and C. Rosenbaum. Legend has it that an

The hopper sits above the grinding stone and is turned by water power to grind corn into meal or grits. The miller at Sciples Water Mill fills large bags with ground corn. *Courtesy of the author.*

Sciples General Store is now a music hall for musicians and music lovers. *Courtesy of the author.*

angry mob of two hundred had taken over the town, and within seventy-five feet of the jail, three fatal bullets found their way into J.P. Gilmer's body. The comments of A. McLelland angered the crowd, and he, too, fell of an assassin's bullet. The deadly fracas continued, and at least three others died in the massacre.[73]

Sciples General Store is now used as a music hall for musicians and music lovers. The building once served as a general store for the community after the original store beside the watermill collapsed from age.

# JEFFERSON DAVIS COUNTY

Jefferson Davis County is named for the only man who served as president of the Confederacy. The county, formed on March 31, 1906, and once rich in yellow pine, was carved from Covington and Lawrence Counties.

## A.F. Carraway General Store
## Bassfield

F. (Augusta Fletcher) Carraway Sr. was born on December 7, 1876, in Holiday Creek, Covington County, Mississippi,[74] and by 1910, the section of the county in which he lived had been included in the newly formed Jefferson Davis County.

In 1919, Carraway opened the A.F. Carraway General Store in Bassfield, and since that time, the doors of this quaint store have remained opened. Two large display windows flank each side of the entrance. I paused for a second, as if to snap a mental image of the worn loafer's bench that sat near the door. I stepped through the double set of screened doors and walked into the past. Rustic wood floors polished from decades of footsteps stretch the length of the room; shelves line the wall; large, heavy tables are centered in the room and filled with a haphazard placement of men's khaki pants, iron skillets and galvanized pails of all sizes; and vintage cash registers are scattered about. On the right, a long counter runs half the length of the building. I hesitated only for a moment because I was eager to explore the old store. I walked across the wood floors, straight to the counter, where a small group of people was chatting, introduced myself and explained my presence before I began to poke around in the store.

Emma, my sister-in-law, had accompanied me on a day trip that would lead to the southwestern corner of the state. She browsed over a selection of metal pails in different sizes, which I assumed she intended to use as flowerpots.

"Do you plan on buying a cow to milk?" I teased.

"We may all need a cow if the price of milk keeps going up," she said.

"Well, don't forget to ask if they sell milk-churns too, because the cost of milk might entice you to churn your own butter." We laughed, and I continued to explore the store while she hand weighed pails.

Timber and agriculture thrived during the early 1900s, and the A.F. Carraway General Store provided staples, farm implements, washtubs, buckets, seeds, cloths and other notions to meet the needs of the community.

Unlike large cities in the North, the Great Depression did not have a tremendously damaging impact on rural communities in the South. Most, if not all, people were farmers who grew and harvested vegetables, raised and slaughtered livestock, milked cows, ground corn into meal, churned butter and used cane or sorghum syrup as a sweetener; even so, life was hard for the farm family during the Depression. Other than a few bare necessities,

Two sets of screened doors lead into the entry of the A.F. Carraway Store in Bassfield. *Courtesy of the author.*

Vintage cash registers once used in the A.F. Carraway Store are scattered about. Iron skillets, metal pails and work pants are displayed on tables centered in the store. A ladder once used by the merchant to reach items from the shelves is still attached to a rod that runs the length of the wall. *Courtesy of the author.*

which were often bartered for, rural farmers faired better than their northern neighbors in large cities.

Farmers taught sons at an early age how to plow, plant and care for livestock. Farm boys hunted wild game, swam in creeks and made brooms from sagebrush to sweep the yard free of grass for Sunday afternoon company. They whittled slingshots from wood, and girls made dolls from clothespins and dressed them from scraps of fabric. Meanwhile, farm mothers were the first to rise in the morning and the last to retire at night, long after children, dressed in "union suits" were snuggled under layers of handmade quilts. Nursing infants interrupted mothers' nights, and their days were filled with chores that began when they stoked the stove with firewood to serve breakfast before the break of dawn. The old adage held true: "A woman's work is never done."

# NOXUBEE COUNTY

Noxubee County formed on December 23, 1833, and derived its name from an Indian word that means "stinking water." The Treaty of Dancing Rabbit Creek was signed in Noxubee County in 1830.

## E.F. Nunn General Store
## Shuqualak

As the encroachment of settlers arrived within the boundaries of Mississippi, a state with navigable waterways, the need for agricultural land grew after the invention of Eli Whitney's cotton gin. President Andrew Jackson's concern for land added another injustice that occurred after slavery was introduced by the French.

On September 27, 1830, representatives of the government and the Choctaws met to sign the Treaty of Dancing Rabbit Creek. Within the Choctaw chiefdom, Greenwood Leflore, Mushulatubbee and Hopaii iskitini, who was known as Little Leader, met with Major John H. Eaton, Colonel John Coffee and the appointed interpreter John Ptchlynn on Choctaw land. When the last signature had been written on the Treaty of Dancing Rabbit Creek, the Choctaw lands had been ceded. This led to the removal of the Choctaws, a people who would walk the Trail of Tears to Oklahoma.

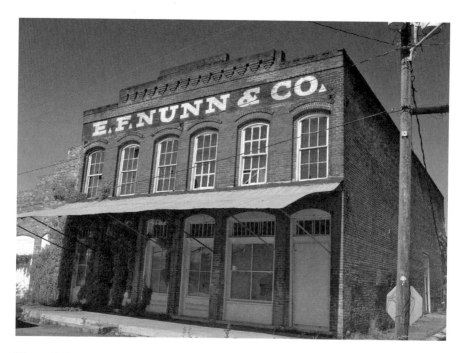

The red brick two-story general store that once belonged to E.L. Nunn in Shuqualak has long since closed its doors. Kudzu, a fast-growing plant, has crept up the brick walls of the store. *Courtesy of the author.*

The creation of Noxubee County would be formed from these Choctaw lands that included the Noxubee River, a county claimed as a hunter's paradise.

Among the setters that arrived in Noxubee County was E.F. (Elisha F.) Nunn, who was born in Oglethorpe County, Georgia, and later settled in Shuqualak. About 1866, he built a two-story red brick general store on the south side of the Mobile & Ohio Railroad track, and by 1870, he owned one of the most prosperous businesses in the village: the E.F. Nunn Company. Elisha and his thirty-seven-year-old wife, Mary, had a one-year-old daughter by the name of Callie. By 1880, he was both a merchant and planter.[75]

Nunn expanded his businesses and began a sawmill that milled Mississippi's gold: the yellow pine. Fire destroyed the mill in the early 1900s.

Like for the rest of the nation, word reached Shuqualak residences when Fred and Al Key's plane the Ole Miss touched down on July 1, 1935, after 653 hours of sustained flight and broke the world record.

In 1948, E.G. Flora, Richard Prince and Charles H. Thomas formed the Shuqualak Lumber Company and produced yellow pine lumber. The blast of the train whistle still alerts the few who live nearby of trains' arrivals;

the doors of most businesses are closed, but the history told to young great-grandsons—of a thriving E.F. Nunn's General Store, the sound of horses, the creak of wagons, the touch of calloused hands and the feel of grit from worn clay-crusted boots—still lingers.

# OKTIBBEHA COUNTY

Before the formation of Oktibbeha County, its land had been situated between that of the Chickasaw and Choctaw Indians. The county derives its name from an area creek and was formed on December 23, 1833.

## Gentry Store
### Oktoc

Enticed by two large springs, many settlers to Oktoc were Presbyterians, who established the first church in Oktibbeha County in 1835. The county formed from ceded Choctaw land and the corners of adjoining counties.[76]

James Nason and his brother Richard were Irish immigrants from County Cork who applied for citizenship in South Carolina in 1789. By 1840, both brothers migrated to Starkville with their families. Family history says that James and his wife, Margaret Montgomery, lived in a cabin where the bank is now located downtown. They are buried in a cement-encased grave at Odd Fellows Cemetery in Starkville.

While the War Between the States raged, slaves combed cotton and spun wool into thread to help clothe Confederate troops. The newly spun material had to be boiled in water mixed with meal and dyed from tree bark: walnut bark for black; maple for purple; cherry, hickory or red oak for red.[77]

Slaves lived in log houses, and beds were built into the corner of the room and covered with mattresses made from dried hay.[78] As the county expanded, farming and dairy communities like that of Oktoc sprang up. Most communities in Mississippi will let their hair down for Country Store Day, and Oktoc is no exception. It's a day of entertainment, food and crafts enjoyed by all.

The Oktoc community center is the location for the annual Country Store Day. The community center is composed of two buildings: the Cumberland Presbyterian Church and a one-room schoolhouse. In 1934, the members

Gentry's Store is in the heart of Oktoc. The store once served the Oktoc community after the original store closed its doors and became the community center. *Courtesy of the author.*

of the community rolled the buildings together to create one structure. The buildings may have been rolled over logs.

From 1932 until the store closed in 1999, the Gentry Store's proprietor, Hilman O. Gentry, served the Oktoc community's immediate needs from Band-Aids to baby chicks ordered by local farmers. The Gentry Store is similar to other country stores built after the 1920s, when transportation to rural areas became more affordable. Without a general store, rural families often traveled miles to purchase necessities. The store is located approximately ten miles southeast of Starkville on the Oktoc Road.

## LAFAYETTE COUNTY

Lafayette County was named for Frenchman the Marques de Lafayette when it was formed on February 9, 1836. It is composed of land ceded by the Chickasaws in the Treaty of Pontotoc. The county is home to the University of Mississippi.

## E.L. Bruce Company Store
### Bruce

E.L. Bruce Company Store sold groceries, furniture and other goods in the hardwood lumber mill town of Bruce.[79] The store was first occupied by Clarence Saunders's grocery. The small community lived by the mill's whistle, which is estimated to have blown over seventy-five thousand times, according to the Bruce Chamber of Commerce.

In 1925, a railway spur line was built to the E.L. Bruce Lumber Mill. The twenty-two-mile railway spur, known as the Scoona Valley Railroad Company, connected to the Illinois Central Railway to transport timber and lumber to and from the mill. The lumber mill is now owned by Weyerhaeuser. In 1927, E.L. Bruce opened the company store that faces the park in downtown Bruce. The building once served as city hall and as a movie theater. The upper level of the store served as a classroom in the 1920s after a fire damaged the school.[80]

The E.L. Bruce Company Store is now a forestry museum located on the north side of the town square in Bruce.

E.L. Bruce Company, once a general store, is located in the town square of Bruce. It is said that the town of Bruce lived by the mill's whistle. *Courtesy of the author.*

## Taylor Grocery and Restaurant
### Taylor

I rounded a curve on County Road 338, and Taylor popped into view, a quaint group of buildings with faded signs. Taylor Grocery and Restaurant is located in the same building that was built by Duff Ragland in about 1889, which later became Gid Hurdle general store. Taylor Grocery and Restaurant now calls this old general store home, a popular place for locals who listen to live music and dine on fried catfish.[81]

Dr. John Taylor, an early pioneer who fought in the War of Independence, was a North Carolinian who traveled over stagecoach roads with his wife, Nancy, to reach Lafayette County.[82] He bought 157.12 acres of Chickasaw land[83] before the treaty with the Chickasaw and erected a water-power

Taylor General Store and Restaurant is located in the quaint town of Taylor. The building has served different merchants over years. *Courtesy of the author.*

The name of this old general store located on the same block as Taylor General Store is not known. Two musicians pose in the doorway of the store for the photographer who does tintype photographs. *Courtesy of the author.*

gristmill on the banks of a river near a village known as Yocona, which now bears the name of the early pioneer, Taylor. This was once a village of farmers who grew cotton carried by mule and wagon to the cotton gin.

The Yocona church was first organized in 1840. Children were taught in a log cabin schoolhouse. The word was scattered in Lafayette County when the Mississippi Railroad began construction; in its path was Yocona. The Mississippi Railroad renamed Yocona, and when the doors of the depot opened in 1858, a shingle displayed the name: Taylor Depot.[84] Farmers and cattlemen, formerly dependent on mules and wagons for transportation of goods, now shipped cotton and cattle by rail.

On his march through Mississippi, Sherman ravaged the community, confiscating food, cattle and valuables. After the war, the price of cotton plummeted. Sharecroppers began to farm plantation land once farmed by slaves. Many plantations established company stores where sharecroppers bought staples and supplies.

It would be twenty-four years before Taylor Depot's name would be changed to Taylor. In 1870, three miles west of Taylor Depot, a train plunged from the trestle into a fifty-foot ravine, and many lives were lost. Nine years later, yellow fever would spread across the village and cause much loss of life among its population.

# CARROLL COUNTY

Carroll County, named for Charles Carrollton, has 634 miles of land and was formed from land ceded by the Choctaws in the Treaty of Dancing Rabbit Creek. Carroll County has many distinguished citizens, including U.S. senator John S. McCain, the son of Admiral John S. McCain Sr.

## Vaiden-Koppel-Hawkins General Mercantile Store Vaiden

Dr. Cowles Meade Vaiden, a Virginian, came to Carroll County in 1837 and became a wealthy land owner and planter in Shongalo. He gave a right of way to the railroad, one mile from Shongalo. It is said that Dr. Vaiden, who was a slaveholder, used his slaves to help lay the tracks. Soon the new community of Vaiden sprang up near the railroad and became a prosperous town in the late 1800s. Vaiden's growth overtook Shongalo, and the two areas would merge as Vaiden.

The town soon became populated with merchants, including Dr. Vaiden, who, it is said, built the two-story brick building that would become the Vaiden-Koppel-Hawkins General Mercantile Store and became a partner in the store. Vaiden grew into a prosperous town.

On the first day of January 1863, Vaiden lay in the direct path of Grierson's Raiders. The Union soldiers looted the town and homes of valuables and livestock before going to Major Koppel's home in Shongalo, where it is said they killed him. It is assumed this is the same man who was a partner in the Vaiden-Koppel-Hawkins General Store in Vaiden.

The Vaiden-Kopprel-Hawkins General Store was once located in Vaiden. *Courtesy of Ronnie Collins.*

## Merrill's General Mercantile Store
### Carrolton

In the early 1800s, Carrolton would become a progressive town aided by the railroad, cottonseed oil mill and cotton gins. A Presbyterian church, an Episcopal church and the Carrolton Baptist Church were established in Carrolton before the war.[85]

Merrill's General Store in Carrolton once sold staples, coffins and furniture. The store is now home to the Senator John McCain Family Museum. *Courtesy of the author.*

The town, which is named for Charles Carroll, would prosper for the next few decades. In the early 1830s, Captain Connell built a general store now known as Merrill's General Store.[86]

The proprietor of the 1834 Carrolton General Store, located on the corner of Jackson and Lexington Streets, emblazoned his sideline trade on the west side of the red brick building. This general mercantile store was built by Captain Connell, but the first deed recorded for the store is that of M.S. Stansbury in 1858.

The general store's architectural flair of embedded millwork and a display of bins that held seeds and nails is a testament to past artisans' craftsmanship. Everything from harnesses to plows to handmade coffins and furniture were built and sold at Merrill's Store. Later, the general store housed the Carrollton Coffin Company that sold coffins and a horse-drawn hearse for hire.[87]

After Reconstruction, in 1886, Carrollton became probably the only place that a deadly massacre began over a can of spilt molasses. It began when Ed and Charley Brown were on their way to make a delivery of molasses. The two brothers, who were of Native American and African heritage, accidently bumped into and spilt the sticky concoction on Robert Moore's clothing.[88] James Liddle, the lawyer friend of Moore, took it upon himself to defend his friend, and

A massacre caused by spilt molasses occurred at the Carroll County Courthouse in Carrolton. *Courtesy of the National Archives.*

on February 12, 1886, he confronted the two brothers. The argument escalated, and the brothers denied the accusation made by Liddle that the molasses had been deliberately spilt on Moore as he passed by. The argument continued later, after Liddle finished his lunch, except this time, Liddle drew his gun. It is not known who drew first, but the fracas left all three men injured.

On March 17, 1886, during the trial of Liddle for attempted murder, the Carroll County Courthouse erupted into bloodshed when fifty or more men crashed through the courthouse doors with guns drawn. Gunfire exploded, aimed at the defendants and black spectators who were in attendance; however, the perpetrators were never identified in the massacre.[89]

These days, nothing much happens in Carrolton. Even the insects seem to be in seclusion since the movie scenes adapted from William Faulkner's *The Reivers* were shot at Captain William Ray's antebellum home and Bingham House on Washington Street.[90]

The former Merrill General Store is now a museum that houses the memorabilia of Senator John McCain's ancestors who lived in Carrolton. John McCain lived there as a small boy with his mother and siblings. [91]

Merrill's General Store is located on the corner of Lexington and Jackson Streets in Carrolton.

# BOLIVAR COUNTY

Bolivar County, formed on February 9, 1836, is located in the Delta. The county seat of government is Cleveland, named for Grover Cleveland, the twenty-second president of the United States. Bolivar County is home to Delta State University.

## Dockery Plantation Commissary

This 1930 gas station and general store located on the Dockery Plantation in Sunflower County was named for Will Dockery, who established the plantation in 1895. The plantation thrived and, at one time, employed over two thousand people. Like many plantations, Dockery didn't pay with U.S. Treasury money, but with its own form of money, which was often made of brass and called doogaloo.

Shown here is the rice washer and baptism pool on the Dockery Plantation. The plantation is said to be the birthplace of the blues and is located near Cleveland. *Courtesy of the author.*

The doogaloo could usually only be spent in company stores, but because of Will Dockery's reputation for fair treatment of his employees, the town of Greenwood accepted the money even though it was not backed by the U.S. Treasury.

By 1900, the plantation thrived, and the Yazoo and Mississippi Railway spur was completed to Dockery for shipment of cotton and produce raised on Dockery Plantation.

Many claim the front porch of the Dockery General Store is the birthplace of the blues. Robert Johnson, known for his musical ability on the guitar, lived near Dockery. It is said Johnson was poisoned and died in a sharecropper's shack near Tallahatchie Flats. He is buried near Greenwood.

# SMITH COUNTY

## Watkins General Store
## Taylorsville

In 1900, the town of Taylorsville moved a few miles southeast to take advantage of the Gulf and Ship Island Railroad that ran through Smith County. Taylorville's most prominent citizen from 1903 until 1930 was John T. Watkins, the proprietor of a general store and editor of a newspaper, the *Taylorsville Signal*. Taylorsville is nestled along Leaf River in Smith County where longleaf, shortleaf and loblolly pines grow. Watkins opened Watkins General Store in Taylorsville in 1901, and then in 1903, he established the *Taylorsville Signal*. Virgil Watkins named his father, James T., as editor in 1905. James served in this newspaper position until his death in 1930. At that time, his two daughters, Hattie and Mamie, assumed responsibility of the newspaper until 1966.

Watkins General Store and the newspaper were located in the same building, which is now a museum for the store and newspaper. The white frame building with a covered porch is an example of the architecture of general stores after the turn of the twentieth century. The building housing the museum is located on the corner of Ford and Eaton Street in Taylorsville.

The Watkins Museum and Taylorsville Signal building displays furnishings from the Watkins Store and the *Taylorville Signal* newspaper. The museum is located in Taylorsville. *Courtesy of the National Archives.*

Sunlight floods the interior of the Watkins Museum and Taylorsville Signal building. The printing press and store fixtures from Watkins General Store is in the museum. *Courtesy of the National Archives.*

# HOLMES COUNTY

## F.M. Clark General Store
### Mileston

Frank M. Clark is listed under a variety of given first names on census records, which may be due to census taker error. Listed on the 1910 federal census, Clark worked as a salesman in a dry goods store in Claiborne County. He is listed on the 1910 federal census with his wife, Norma M.; daughter Frances M.; and son Frank M.

He continued to work as a salesman in Claiborne County until 1920. He prospered and hired a cook, Irene Luster, for his wife, Norma M., and children Frank M., Frances M. and Elma S.

By 1930, Frank and his family lived in Holmes County, where he retired as a store merchant. He died sometime before 1940, and his wife, Norma, continued as postmaster at Mileston. She earned $600 in 1940 as postmaster. Their son Frank M. was a farmer in Holmes County. F.M. Clark General Store and Post Office was located at Mileston in Holmes County. The store might have been located on a plantation.

# ITAWAMBA COUNTY

## Jim "Buck" Murphy Store

Jim "Buck" Murphy Store is a museum that depicts the general store of the late 1800s. The museum is built in the exact location of the original general store, which served the community of people who lived and worked on farms. The museum includes the furnishings of the original store; its purpose is to represent the rural life in which the general store and church were an important part of the community. The Jim "Buck" Murphy store has appeared on album and CD covers and is located at 1454 Murphy Road, Mantachie.

The Jim "Buck" Murphy Store is a museum that displays the original early 1900s general store fixtures. *Courtesy of Marian Lyle.*

Hopson Plantation Commissary has been transformed into a restaurant and musical entertainment establishment located near Clarksdale. *Courtesy of Robert Birdsong.*

# Coahoma County

## Hopson Plantation Company Store
## Clarksdale

The Hopson Plantation planted its roots in the county when fields were plowed with mules and horses. Hopson Plantation was first farm in the nation to produce crops with the use of International Harvester's cotton picker. Hopson Plantation's commissary has been transformed into a popular spot for dining and music entertainment. The Shack Up Inn, which is part of the old Hopson Plantation, rents sharecropper cabins to overnight guests.

# 6

# MISSISSIPPI LEGENDS

Myths and legends will continue to grow. Juzon (also spelled Juzan) Lake, Murrell, the Gold Hole, Mason and the Harpes are all examples of some of the most famous myths. Many are oral folktales that arrived with settlers from Europe that have been embellished and retold time and again. One such legend in particular is Juzon Lake's ghost lights, which in all probability is an atmospheric condition associated with the lake. Lights such as these have been reported elsewhere in the South. The legend of Juzon is probably an embellished folktale that originated with Irish settlers in Newton County during the early 1800s, a myth that has grown to include Juzon and a nameless Indian.

It is not likely that Juzon committed the deeds of which he was accused, since he was a prominent man who hosted the Choctaw Academy in his home. The school had been established to acquaint the Choctaw with the white man's ways.[92]

A few years before Juzon's death, he became a Choctaw chief, according to the *Chronicles of Oklahoma*.

During the mid-1800s in Choctaw County, according to J.P. Coleman's *Chronicles of Choctaw County*, people visited one another's homes and tried to contact the spiritual world. Voodoo existed among Africans who were brought here and sold into slavery, although plantation owners had prohibited the practice. Do I believe an element of truth is buried in legends? Perhaps.

# 7

# A PLACE CALLED MISSISSIPPI

Hundreds of flatboats with merchandise have floated down the Mississippi River. Boatmen returned by an old Indian trail now known as the Natchez Trace. Many travelers on the footpath were robbed by Samuel Mason and two cutthroat bandits, Micjah and Wiley Harp. The gang continued to terrorize kaintucks, boatmen who used flatboats to transport goods, on the footpath, and few, if any, who encountered the murderous gang survived.

Governor Claiborne posted a bounty on the head of Samuel Mason, dead or alive. One of Mason's gang members planned to claim the bounty by cutting off the head of an innocent man and presenting it to the governor as though it belonged to the infamous highwayman. After the deceit was discovered, the culprits were hanged at Greenville at a site known as Gallows Field.[93]

It is said that the two notorious bandits Michjah and Wiley Harpe tortured or hacked their human prey into pieces and then made their way to Cave in the Rock in Illinois to meet Samuel Mason, the notorious Natchez Trace bandit. It is also said that Mason turned the two thieving killers away.[94]

The legend continued to fracture and grow with each embellishment of the three most notorious and dangerous men on the Natchez Trace: Samuel Mason, Michjah and Wiley Harpe.

These are the legendary rumors spun in Mississippi before yellow fever struck its blow in Greenville and before Holt Collier, who had been a slave since the moment he entered this world in 1846. Collier, a sharpshooter and cavalryman for the Confederacy, is the man who later captured a bear near Onward for Theodore Roosevelt's bear hunt. Holt Collier died in 1936, shortly before the great flood—when the Mississippi River broke its levee at Mound Landing on April 21, 1927—decimated Greenville. Holt Collier is buried at Greenville's Live Oak Cemetery.

In the early 1800s, when the notorious land pirate John A. Merrell and his gang terrorized the Mississippi Territory, Merrell was considered the most dangerous and feared river pirate and highwayman in the Natchez district.

# IN REMEMBRANCE

## The Early Days of Mississippi

Relax. Close your eyes for a moment and imagine a time long forgotten. Do you hear voices, English and foreign, mingle? Open your eyes and look beyond the fort—over there, below the bluff, where river boatmen scurry about unloading cargo. Hurry now, merge with the boatmen near the trading post; a French solider is near, his hand on his sheath ready to draw his sword.

Step inside the trading post built from hand-hewn logs. Do you see the beaver pelts stacked in the corner? Watch the exchange between a boatman and the trader; see how he examines each pelt? Don't let the odor of animal pelts overcome you—step outside. Watch the men dismantle flatboats. Do you see the Indian with a basket of corn approach a boatman and make the exchange?

The sun drifts low in the horizon. The sky deepens to a rose hue that spreads across a darkening sky.

The day has quieted to a hum, and twilight has descended. Campfires are aglow. Laughter and voices drift over the river while wild game and corn are cooked over a campfire.

Morning dew glistens on foliage, and the chill of fear hangs in the air. Follow the traders down the footpath; you're homeward bound. Watch your step, and stay alert for bandits and bears.

Close your eyes again and relax.

Walk just beyond the gristmill and wagonloads of corn, past the old-timers who swap tales on the loafer's bench. Open the screen door of the general store, and step inside. Listen to the door creak to a close on rusted hinges.

Now, reach out and let your fingers caress the smooth mahogany and glass display case near the door, and then touch the rough wood of ceiling-high shelves that line the wall. Walk past the potbellied stove, iron wash pots, pails and plows and the bins of nails and seeds. Step toward the wooden barrel in the corner, the one that holds peanuts. Imagine the taste if you were parched, how it tantalizes the tongue; sit in the barber chair tucked into the corner, and listen to the sounds of the past.

Follow the mellow waft of hoop cheese that drifts throughout the store. Savor a stick of licorice candy from the wide-mouth jar, and listen to the farmer as he places his order with the store clerk.

Watch how smooth the ladder rolls along the wall, past the tin containers sold to hold rendered lard. Do you hear the creak of the ladder rungs as the clerk climbs up to fetch the fifty-pound bag of flour from the shelf, and did you feel the weight as the clerk hoisted the bag over his shoulder to descend the ladder?

Did you notice how comfortable your worn boots are and how cool faded overalls are? Go ahead, hook your finger around the metal clasp while you visualize a time from long ago. Smell the fresh scent of hay in the barn; listen to the sound of a rooster crow at dawn. Listen to the children's laughter as they splash in the cool creek waters of the Chickasawhay. Imagine your place at the Sunday dinner table filled with a bounty of farm-raised food; wash it down with a glass of milk from a crock chilled in the well.

Taste the fresh ground meal baked into bread in a wood stove, and savor the molasses poured over hot buttered biscuits. Tease your senses with the aroma of hickory smoked bacon and ham. Bow your head and listen to a father's prayer. Enjoy the family's chatter around the breakfast table before church, followed by an afternoon of fellowship with friends and family on the front porch. It's a time to spin tales of local legends, and no one—not even you—will know if they are true.

Open your eyes; you're in a modern-day convenience store. It's doubtful the store will evoke the same feelings you've experienced in country stores in Mississippi.

Today, many of the remaining country stores have been turned into restaurants and antique shops, but even so, the architecture of these few stores stand as a remembrance to our historical past.

# NOTES

1. U.S. National Park Service, "Natchez Trace: Kaintucks."
2. Libby, *Slavery and Frontier Mississippi*.
3. Barnett, "Yamasee War," 2–13.
4. Libby, *Slavery and Frontier Mississippi*.
5. U.S. National Park Service, "Natchez Trace: Kaintucks."
6. Libby, *Slavery and Frontier Mississippi*.
7. U.S. National Park Service, "Mississippi River Facts."
8. Fulkerson, *Random Recollections*, 25.
9. Gardner, *Natchez Trace*.
10. Monette, *History of the Discovery and Settlement of the Valley of the Mississippi*."
11. Langley, "Malmaison."
12. Libby, *Slavery and Frontier Mississippi*.
13. Journal of the Confederate Congress, 497.
14. Ibid., 496.
15. PBS, Reconstruction.
16. Application for Historic Buildings, "E.W. Hagwood General Store."
17. Hagwood and Sellers, personal interview.
18. Mosley, personal interview.
19. Culpepper, personal interview.
20. Record of Postmaster Appointments, Joseph Thornton Gunn, 17:728.
21. Davis, telephone interview.
22. Record of Postmaster Appointments, John McElroy, 83:144.
23. Henry, WPA Slave Narrative.
24. Ibid.
25. Record of Postmaster Appointments, Jubal B. Hancock.

26. White, "Marion Brick Yard Gunfight."

27. Ibid.

28. Ibid.

29. Hancock, U.S. House of Representative Private Claims, 178, 837.

30. Maloney, *Meridian, Mississippi City Directory*.

31. Pollard, "All This Happened at Bovina Crossing."

32. Ibid.

33. Ibid.

34. Sharkey, *Goodspeed*, 204–05.

35. Ibid.

36. U.S. National Park Service, "Mound Builders."

37. Ibid.

38. U.S. Bureau of the Census, Dr. William T. Street.

39. Ibid.

40. Record of Postmaster Appointments, Robert Ross.

41. Holmes, "Choctaw Stickball."

42. Clarke, "History of Clark County."

43. Allen, BLM Certificate, 253:134.

44. Record of Postmaster Appointments, Stephen Jellenc, 3:48.

45. Mallard and Mallard, "Brief History of Enterprise."

46. Hunter, personal interview.

47. Ibid.

48. Record of Postmaster Appointments, Vida A. Keeton, 45:642.

49. Moore, "Girls' Tomato Clubs."

50. Fulkerson, *Random Recollections*, 6.

51. U.S. Bureau of the Census, Berthold Lohmann; Carl Lohmann.

52. Rowland, *History of Hinds County*, 12.

53. *Oxford American*, So Lost: Harris Carmichael Store.

54. Pate, "Leflore."

55. Federal Bureau of Investigation, Emmett Till, 6.

56. Ibid., 20.

57. Ibid., 40.

58. Ibid., 8.

59. Ibid., 1.

60. Ibid., 39.

61. Rowland, *Mississippi*.

62. Howell, *Mississippi Home-places*, 38.

63. Gould, *Fifty Years on the Mississippi*, 73.

64. Ibid., 160–61.

65. Fulkerson, *Random Recollections*, 38.

66. Mitcham, *Old Rodney*, 243.

67. Nutt, "Pilgrimage Historical Association Collection: Nutt Family Papers."

68. *Fayette Chronicle*, September 8, 1958.
69. Ibid.
70. W.F. Rodgers, National Register of Historic Places Nomination Form.
71. U.S. Bureau of the Census, W.F. Rodgers.
72. Clark, *Bloody Kemper*.
73. Journal of the Confederate Congress, 497.
74. Ancestry.com, U.S., WWI Civilian Draft Registrations.
75. U.S. Bureau of the Census, E.F. Nunn.
76. Gibbs, WPA Slave Narrative.
77. Ibid.
78. Ibid.
79. McNeese, Joel, *Calhoun County Journal*, March 30, 2011.
80. Ibid.
81. Taylor Grocery and Restaurant.
82. TaylorHistory.org.
83. Allen, BLM Certificate, 285:208
84. Taylor Grocery and Restaurant; TaylorHistory.org.
85. *Biographical and Historical Memoirs*, 284.
86. Merrills General Mercantile, National Register of Historic Places Nomination Form.
87. Ibid.
88. Ward, "Carroll County Courthouse Massacre."
89. Ibid.
90. Carroll County, Mississippi Genealogy & History Network.
91. McMillin, "McCain Family."
92. Langley, "Malmaison."
93. Lowry and McCardle, *History of Mississippi*, 502–07.
94. Daniels, *Devil's Backbone*, 20.

# BIBLIOGRAPHY

Abraham Lincoln Historical Digitization Project. Northern Illinois University Libraries Digitization Projects. http://lincoln.lib.niu.edu/cgi-bin/philologic/getobject.pl?c.1001:12.lincoln (accessed December 12, 2011).

Allen, Susan. BLM Certificate No. 10731.

Ancestry.com. U.S., WWI Civilian Draft Registrations, 1917–1918.

Application for Historic Building. "E.W. Hagwood General Store." Nomination Form.

Army Corp of Engineers. Mississippi River Navigation, 1985. U.S. Army Corps of Engineers New Orleans District. http://www.mvn.usace.army.mil/pao/history/MISSRNAV/index.asp (accessed January 29, 2012).

Barnett, James F., Jr. "The Yamasee War, the Bearded Chief, and the Founding of Fort Rosalie." http://mdah.state.ms.us/new/wp-content/uploads/2013/07/JMH_Spring2012.pdf (accessed November 4, 2013).

Bienville, Jean Baptiste le Moyne de. mdah.state.ms.us/timeline/people/jean-baptiste-lemoyne-sieur-de-bienville/ (accessed May 9, 2013).

*Biographical and Historical Memoirs of Mississippi*. Vol. 1, part 2. Gretna, LA: Pelican Publishing Company, n.d.

Bozman, Kelli. "Where in Mississippi Is Onward?" Editorial. *Mississippi Magazine*, September 1, 2002. http://thefreelibrary.com (accessed December 19, 2011).

Buck, Ronnie, Randall Mauck and Johnnie Mauck. Personal interview. June–July 2010.

Carroll County, Mississippi Genealogy & History Network. www.carroll.msghn.org (accessed July 5, 2011).

Carter, Lucy. Personal interview. August 2011.

Chapman, Beth. "Legend of the Gold Hole." *Daily (Brookhaven) Leader,* June 26, 2000.

Clarke, Joshua G. "History of Clarke County and Its Municipalities." www. clarkecountychamber.com/HISTORY.html (accessed January 6, 2012).

Clark, Hewitt. *Bloody Kemper: A True Story in Mis'sippi.* Spring, TX: Lone Star Press, 1998.

Clark, Obie. "Oral History Transcripts: Obie Clark." Interview by Donald Williams. University of Southern Mississippi, October 25, 2003. www.usm. edu/crdp/html/transcripts/clark_obie.shtml (accessed December 13, 2011).

Culpepper, Joanne Hagwood. Personal interview. June 2011.

Cushman, H.B. *History of the Choctaw, Chickasaw, and Natchez Indians.* Greenville, MS: Headlight Printing House, 1899.

Cushman, H.B., and Angie Debo. *History of the Choctaw, Chickasaw, and Natchez Indians.* Norman: University of Oklahoma Press, 1999.

Daniels, Jonathan. *The Devil's Backbone: The Story of the Natchez Trace.* Reprint. Gretna, LA: Pelican Publishing Company, 1998.

Davis, Harlan. Telephone interview. December 4, 2011.

De Grand Pre, Carlos. "List of Tobacco Growers in 1790 Spanish Natchez District." http://www.natchezbelle.org/sw/tobaccogrowers1790.htm.

Dewan, Shaila, and Ariel Hart. "F.B.I. Discovers Trial Transcript in Emmett Till Case." *New York Times,* May 18, 2005. www.nytimes.com/2005/05/18/ national/18till.html (accessed December 12, 2011).

*Fayette Chronicle,* September 8, 1958.

Federal Bureau of Investigation. Emmett Till. Vol. 1. FBI: The Vault. http:// vault.fbi.gov (accessed January 15, 2012).

Fort Rosalie Gift Shop. 500 South Canal Street, Natchez, Adams, Mississippi. Library of Congress American Memory. http://memory.loc.gov/cgi- bin/query (accessed December 17, 2011).

Fulkerson, H.S. *Random Recollections of Early Days in Mississippi.* N.p., 1972.

Gardner, Malcolm. *The Natchez Trace: An Historical Parkway.* Vol. 2. Ser. 4. National Park Service Cultural Resources Discover History. www.cr.nps.gov/history/ online_books/regional_review/vol2-4d.htm (accessed December 12, 2011).

GenDisasters. "Kewanee, MS Express and Freight Collision, March 1904." Submitted by Stu Beitler. August 30, 2010. www3.gendisasters. com/mississippi/17030/kewanee-ms-express-freight-collision-mar-1904 (accessed October 24, 2011).

Gibbs, Henry. WPA Slave Narrative. Library of Congress.

Gould, Emmerson (E.W.). *Fifty Years on the Mississippi; or, Gould's History of River Navigation....* St. Louis, MO: Nixon-Jones Print Co., 1889.

Hagwood, Dorothy T., Caroline Smith and Joann H. Culpepper. Personal interview. April 9, 2009.

Hagwood, Dorothy T., Leslie Haugewood, Joann H. Culpepper, Carolyn Smith and Sharon Hurt. Personal interview. April 4, 2008.

Hagwood, Leslie, and Alan Sellers. Personal interview. Spring 1980.

Hancock, Jubal B. U.S. House of Representative Private Claims. Vol. 2.

Henry, Nettie. WPA Slave Narrative, Meridian, Lauderdale County. Library of Congress.

Holmes, Baxter. "Choctaw Stickball: A Fierce, Ancient Game Deep in Mississippi." *LA Times*, October 18, 2011. http://articles.latimes.com/2011/oct/18/nation/la-na-choctaw-stickball-20111019.

Howell, Elmo. *Mississippi Home-places: Notes on Literature and History*. Memphis, TN: E. Howell, 1988.

Hughes, Odell. "Paulding." RootsWeb.com Home Page. www.rootsweb.ancestry.com/~msjasper/community/commpaulding.html (accessed November 14, 2011).

Huie, William Bradford. "The Shocking Story of Approved Killings in Mississippi." *Look Magazine*, January 24, 1956.

Hunter, Johnny. Personal interview, n.d.

Journal of the Confederate Congress, December 30, 1863. Vol. 3.

Langley, Mrs. Lee J. "Malmaison, Palace in a Wilderness: Home of General Leflore, Mississippi's Remarkable Indian Statesman." *Chronicles of Oklahoma* 5, no. 4. Oklahoma City: Oklahoma Historical Society, 2001. http://digital.library.okstate.edu/Chronicles/v005/v005p371.html.

Libby, David J. *Slavery and Frontier Mississippi, 1720–1835*. Jackson: University of Mississippi Press, 2004.

Lowry, Robert, and William H. McCardle. *A History of Mississippi: From the Discovery of the Great River…* Jackson, MS: R.H. Henry & Company, 1891.

Mallard, Joe Robert, and Mary Margaret Mallard. "A Brief History of Enterprise, Clark Co., Mississippi." May 10, 1996. http://www.oocities.org/hattiesburg_history/enterprise.html.

Maloney, T.V., ed. *Meridian, Mississippi City Directory, Metropolis of the Southwest: A Descriptive, Historical and Statistical Review; Industry, Development, and Enterprise, 1888*. Privately printed.

McMillin, Zack. "McCain Family Has Deep Mississippi Roots." *Commercial Appeal*, September 24, 2008.

McNeese, Joel. *Calhoun County Journal*, March 30, 2011.

Merrills General Mercantile, National Register for Historic Places Nomination Form.

Middleton, Richard, and Anne S. Lombard. *Colonial America: A History to 1763*. Chichester, West Sussex, UK: Wiley-Blackwell, 2011.

Mississippi Department of Archives and History. "Governor Jean Baptiste Le Moyne De Bienville." Mississippi History Time Line. http://mdah.state.ms.us/timeline/people/jean-baptiste-lemoyne-sieur-de-bienville.

Mitcham, Howard. *Old Rodney: A Mississippi Ghost Town*. Mississippi Department of Archives and History. http://mdah.state.ms.us/pubs/rodney.pdf.

Monette, John W., MD. *History of the Discovery and Settlement of the Valley of the Mississippi, by the Three Great Eurpoean Powers, Spain, France, and Great Britain, and the Subsequent Occupation, Settlement, and Extension of Civil Government by the United Sates until the Year 1846*. Vol. 1. New York: Harper and Brothers, 1846.

———. "XIII." In *History of the Discovery and Settlement of the Valley of the Mississippi, by the Three Great European Powers, Spain, France, and Great Britain, and the Subsequent Occupation, Settlement and Extension of Civil Government by the United States until the Year 1846*. Vol. 2. New York: Harper & Bros., 1846.

Moore, Danny. "Girls' Tomato Clubs in Mississippi 1911–1915." MsHistorynow.mdah.state.ms.us.

Moore, Robert. Personal interview. November 7, 2011.

Moore, Sue, ed. The MSGenweb Project, n.d. Accessed May 11, 2013.

Mosley, Ethel. Personal interview and access to Mosley's General Store ledger. August 14, 2010.

Nelson, Stanley, prod. PBS American Experience. *The Murder of Emmett Till*. People & Events. www.pbs.org/wgbh/amex/till/peopleevents/p_defendants.html (accessed October 24, 2011).

———. PBS American Experience. *The Murder of Emmett Till*. Transcript. www.pbs.org/wgbh/amex/till/filmmore/pt.html (accessed December 12, 2011).

Nutt, Haller. "Pilgrimage Historical Association Collection: Nutt Family Papers." Mississippi Department of Archives and History. http://mdah.state.ms.us/manuscripts/z1817.html

*Oxford American*. So Lost: Carmichael Store. Video series. October 6, 2009. www.oxfordamerican.org/articles/sections/solost/?page=9.

Pate, James P. "Leflore, Greenwood 1800–1865." Oklahoma Historical Society's Encyclopedia of Oklahoma History & Culture. http://digital.library.okstate.edu/encyclopedia/entries/L/LE008.html (accessed December 29, 2012).

PBS. Reconstruction in Mississippi 1870 timeline. www.pbs.org/wgbh/amex/reconstruction/states/sf_timeline2.html (accessed September 5, 2013).

Pollard, Bob. "All This Happened at Bovina Crossing." http://mysummertree.com/final.pdf.

Record of Postmaster Appointments. 1832–September 30, 1971. Roll 68, Archive Publication M841. National Archives and Records Administration (NARA), Washington, D.C.

Rowland, Dunbar. *Mississippi, Comprising Sketches of Counties, Towns, Events, Institutions, and Persons*. Vol. 1. Atlanta, GA: Southern Historical, 1907.

# BIBLIOGRAPHY

Rowland, Mrs. Dunbar (Eron Opha Rowland). *History of Hines County, Mississippi, 1821–1922*. Jackson, MS: Jones Printing Company, 1922. E-book accessed via the Library of Congress.

"Rural Electrification." New Deal Network. http://newdeal.feri.org/tva/tva10.htm (accessed December 18, 2011).

Sharkey, William Lewis. *Goodspeed*. Vol. 1. N.p.

Sibley, Marlo. "The Heartland." In *Mississippi: Off the Beaten Path*. Old Saybrook, CT: Globe Pequot, 1996.

Taylor Grocery and Restaurant, Taylorgrocery.com.

TaylorHistory.org.

"Teal's Onward Store: Bear Hunt." Teal's Onward Store: Home of the Teddy Bear. http://onward-store.com/bear_hunt.html (accessed December 20, 2011).

U.S. Bureau of the Census. Augustus Franklin Carraway. Year: 1910; Census Place: Beat 3, Jefferson Davis, Mississippi; Roll: T624_744; Page: 26A; Enumeration District: 0069; FHL microfilm: 1374757.

———. Berthold Lohmann. Year: 1900; Census Place: New Orleans Ward 1, Orleans, Louisiana; Roll: 570; Page: 9B; Enumeration District: 0005; FHL microfilm: 1240570.

———. Carl Lohmann. Year: 1900; Census Place: Beat 2, Franklin, Mississippi; Roll: 807; Page: 9A; Enumeration District: 0050; FHL microfilm: 1240807.

———. Dr. William T. Street. Year: 1910; Census Place: Jasper County.

———. E.F. Nunn. Year: 1880; Census Place: Beat 4, Noxubee, Mississippi; Roll: 660; Family History Film: 1254660; Page: 224B; Enumeration District: 032; Image: 0310.

———. Elisha F. Nunn. Year: 1870; Census Place: Township 13, Noxubee, Mississippi; Roll: M593_743; Page: 36A; Image: 75; Family History Library Film: 552242.

———. W.F. Rodgers. Year: 1930; Census Place: Beat 2, Kemper County; Roll: 1152; Page: 11B.

U.S. Department of Agriculture. "USDA Rural Development: UEP Home." Utilities. www.rurdev.usda.gov/UEP_HomePage.html (accessed December 19, 2011).

"The US50: A Guide to the State of Mississippi History." The US50: A Guide to the Fifty States. www.theus50.com/mississippi/history.php (accessed December 12, 2011).

U.S. National Park Service. "Mississippi River Facts." www.nps.gov/miss/riverfacts.htm (accessed November 23, 2012).

———. "The Mound Builders." Indian Mounds of Mississippi. http://www.nps.gov/nr/travel/mounds/builders.htm.

————. Natchez National Historical Park. "Frequently Asked Questions." http://www.nps.gov/natc/faqs.htm (accessed February 17, 2012).

————. "Natchez Trace: Choctaw." http://www.nps.gov/natr/historyculture/choctaw.htm (accessed February 13, 2012).

————. "Natchez Trace: Kaintucks." http://www.nps.gov/natr/historyculture/kaintuck.htm (accessed February 13, 2012).

————. "Natchez Trace Parkway." http://www.nps.gov/natr/index.htm (accessed October 12, 2011).

————. Survey of Historic Sites and Buildings. www.nps.gov/history/history/online_books/explorers/intro.htm (accessed December 12, 2011).

Ward, Rick. "The Carroll County Courthouse Massacre, 1886: A Cold Case File." mshistorynow.mdah.state.ms.us/articles/381/the-carroll-county-courthouse-massacre-1886-a-cold-case-file.

W.F. Rogers General Store, National Register of Historic Places Nomination Form.

White, Bill. "The Marion Brick Yard Gunfight." Lauderdale County Genealogy Web. www.lauderdalecoms.com/exclusivearticles/mariongunfight.htm (accessed January 2, 2014).

Wikipedia. "Fort Rosalie." http://en.wikipedia.org/wiki/Fort_Rosalie (accessed February 17, 2012).

*The WPA Guide to the Magnolia State.* Jackson: University of Mississippi Press, 2009.

Wright, Gerald W., Sr., and Gary Pickett. Personal interview. August 8, 2010.

# INDEX

# INDEX

# INDEX

# ABOUT THE AUTHOR

June Davis Davidson was born in Lakeland, Florida, but she has resided in Mississippi for over fifty years. She is listed on the Mississippi Arts Commission as a literary artist. June is a member of the Mississippi Alliance for Arts Education and the Mississippi Writers' Guild, where she has also served as board member. She is the author of two previously published nonfiction books. June's fond memories of a historic country store in the community where she and her husband, Bobby, live is the inspiration that led to this book.